U.S. FOREIGN POLICY AND EUROPEAN SECURITY

Also by Arthur Cyr
LIBERAL PARTY POLITICS IN BRITAIN
BRITISH FOREIGN POLICY AND THE ATLANTIC AREA

U.S. FOREIGN POLICY AND EUROPEAN SECURITY

Arthur Cyr
Vice President and Program Director
The Chicago Council on Foreign Relations

MACMILLAN
PRESS

First published 1987

Published by
THE MACMILLAN PRESS LTD
Houndmills, Basingstoke, Hampshire RG21 2XS
and London
Companies and representatives
throughout the world

Printed in Hong Kong

British Library Cataloguing in Publication Data
Cyr, Arthur
U.S. Foreign policy and European Security.
1. North Atlantic Treaty Organization – History
I. Title
355'.031'091821   UA646.3
ISBN 0–333–32859–0

To Jamie, Tom and David – the last is first

Contents

1 Introduction

The purpose of this extended essay is to provide discussion and, ideally, insight concerning a variety of the principal problems currently facing the North Atlantic Treaty Organization – the Atlantic Alliance – along with some evaluation of suggested changes in both policies and goals. The subject is both old and new, which means that some effort is required to put the conventional wisdom in current focus, respond to the challenges of a shifting international environment, and address in particular the issue of how appropriate existing relationships are in the context of the contemporary international system. There is a considerable existing literature on Alliance issues. The security of Europe, the insecurity of the borders dividing East from West, the exposed political nerve represented by Berlin – these elements have been the preoccupation and source of tensions in Soviet–American relations since the beginning of the Cold War. There is no shortage of studies of the bases of this most fundamental, stark and far-reaching ideological conflict in the modern international system.

This particular study is designed to place contemporary debates and suggestions in the wider historical context of the development of the Alliance from the beginning. I hope that the chapters which follow will contribute in a useful manner to debate over United States foreign policy toward Europe. In many ways, the debate over the state of the Alliance has grown rather steadily more intense over approximately the past decade. The reasons for this are understandable but also complex, and not all of the concern voiced about the problems of the Alliance has been truly merited or representative of the realities of the situation.

The subject is in part not new, of course, because the Alliance is not new. Nato is in fact one of the longest-lasting regional security pacts in history. The fact that the partners have been able to maintain formal institutional cohesion, and regional political co-operation as well, since the formation of the Alliance in 1949 is a major accomplishment and stands as such without reference to other developments. Success has resulted in numerous and varied treatments of the subject, often urgent and crisis-oriented in earlier years, more recently taking the longer time perspective available and arguing that gradual decay is taking place in Nato.

The most telling single fact about the Atlantic Alliance, developed over the course of this book, is that institutional and political survival does not imply the absence of, but rather the management of, a series of important internal strains. From the start of Nato, a wide variety of differences in national interests and outlooks have generated conflicts. Important issues have involved the basic, continued European dependence on the nuclear umbrella of the American superpower. More recent difficulties have reflected the economic revival of Europe and consequent waning of American dominance, continuation of differences of view on 'third areas' of the world in a time of greater European independence, Soviet mischief in trying to exploit these differences and enlarge policy fissures, and other factors. Continuity has of course been present as well, from the American perspective most notably in the fact that Nato has been the institutional centre-piece of post-Second World War foreign policy, however such developments as *détente* with the Soviet Union or war in Indochina have distracted attention for certain periods of time.

At the same time, a variety of considerations lead to the conclusion that the subject nevertheless still deserves more attention. First, the political environments of Western and Eastern Europe have been changing. Though the national borders in Europe remain fixed, diplomatic currents have become increasingly fluid. If conflict is constant, the nature of conflicts – their genesis and directions – has changed. Even the political significance of borders has been altered, at times with dramatic result. Notable in this regard is both the *Ostpolitik* of the West German goverment in the late 1960s and early 1970s, and the Helsinki accords of the mid-1970s. Their regularization of relations with the Soviet bloc has not ended the Cold War but has in important ways altered the board on which the game is played.

Second, recent years have witnessed some major shifts in the relationship between the United States and the Soviet Union. Two Republican administrations, under Presidents Nixon and Reagan, have initiated two very different sorts of broad stance toward the adversary superpower, representing in each case dramatic shifts from the *status quo*. *Détente* was the great achievement of Nixon and Kissinger, involving not only the comprehensive strategic nuclear-arms agreements contained in the Salt I treaties, but also extensive economic, scientific and other technical understandings. This has been followed under Reagan by a massive military build-up, designed directly to counter the enormous cumulative Soviet military expansion of the past two decades. The Soviet efforts have been perceived to be so threatening as to promise a fundamental shift in the balance of military power between East and West; indeed, some conservatives have argued for some time that such a shift has actually taken place. Moreover, there was by the early 1980s a consensus clearly reaching beyond the far right that the Soviet threat was so enhanced that greater military efforts by the West were required. It was, after all, the Carter Administration that began to reverse the course of steady or declining real spending on defence during the 1970s. That Democratic administration also took the lead in securing Nato agreement that the partners to the Alliance would each endeavour to increase military spending by 3 per cent in real terms annually. The Reagan Administration has carried the process further, more clearly and with more enthusiasm than the previous regime.

Third, over the past decade there has been a great shift in the mix of elements which comprise security for both the nation states and the larger Alliance structure. After more than twenty years of focus on straightforward military weapons and manpower issues during the period of the long post-war economic boom, the situation has now changed dramatically. The Opec (Organization of Petroleum Exporting Countries) price shocks of 1973–74 were an indication in the starkest possible terms that economic questions were becoming more consequential to international politics even as the answers became more uncertain. And these were only one set of indicators of change among a variety available.

The years of steady, comparatively easy economic growth in the West, with low unemployment and low inflation, stable trade flows and fixed monetary values have come to an end. We now live in a period of much greater economic uncertainty. Trade and monetary frictions have come to pit military allies against one another in economic competition, and have threatened a return to the devastating protectionism, undercutting currency devaluations and escalating trade walls of the Great Depression of the 1930s. The economic base upon which military strength has been built is no longer quite as stable, reliable and predictable. Opec policies demonstrated the fragile character of the supply of the most fundamental commodity of the industrial system of the modern world – petroleum. In effect, a number of economic uncertainties must be added to the international security mix, complicating calculations by policy-markers and requiring that different, more numerous and more unfamiliar elements be related to one another in conceptual terms.

Japan represents a special case in this particular context. With limited but growing military capabilities, the Japanese have also managed to establish their nation as a genuine superpower in economic terms. They have displayed a remarkable capacity to compete with the main industrial nations of the West, including the United States. They have penetrated effectively into a number of markets, capturing large shares in textiles, steel, automobiles, televisions and, increasingly, advanced electronics of various kinds. Trilateralism became fashionable as a result of the realization by informed, influential people in Europe and North America that Japan represents a comparable third base of power and influence, one which more than compensates in economic scale and inpact for what is so far lacking on the military front. By economic indices, the Japanese are not only on a par with the Americans and the Europeans, but have surpassed the latter and are locked in an intense, wide-ranging, ruthless competition with the former. What are the implications of this important development for the Atlantic Alliance?

In consideration of these developments, there are a number of comparatively urgent questions bearing upon the Alliance. Should Nato be expanded in responsibilities to include economic co-ordination? Should the Japanese, already steadily increasing their military capabilities, be encouraged not only to go further down that road but also formally to join the Alliance? Does comparability in level of industrial and technological development, along with shared perspectives on the character of the Soviet threat, outweigh problems of geography and lingering Japanese anti-militarism? If not formal membership in Nato, are there other specific mechanisms which could be exploited in order to gain greater co-operation between Atlantic nations and this Pacific-based economic superpower? Should American institutional priorities be reoriented more explicitly toward Asia, the scene of the United States' last three wars? In sum, is a shifting relationship between the United States and Japan a source of competition for American Alliance attention, of possible greater co-operation within the Atlantic Alliance, or of both – or neither?

Fourth, consideration of the current state of affairs in Nato leads into discussion of various practical remedies. In this context, there remains considerable room for discussion and analysis of drastic departures from the *status quo* in strategies, troops and weapons profiles as well as forms of organization. To generalize, most existing studies of Nato and related political and security issues emphasize adjustments at the margins, incremental changes, or – at the other extreme – thorough alterations of the present situation. This is understandable, given that the *status quo* in Europe has generally been unchanged for more than three decades. Should this approach be replaced, or at least complemented, by more drastic remedies?

The direct confrontation between the two superpowers and their respective blocs of allies prevents much diplomatic movement, and the elaborate institutional and bureaucratic superstructure which supports the Alliance has been in place for a long period of time. For this very reason, there is a tendency simply to reinforce the *status quo*, extrapolating current arrangements into the future. Alternatively, there is an incentive, in the interest of freshness and reform, to propose drastic alterations in the *status quo*. Consequently, there has been considerable discussion of potentials for using Nato to handle, in formal institutional terms, conflicts in third areas outside Western Europe and North America. The oil crisis of the 1970s, and continuing tensions in the Middle East and Gulf region, have been one rather obvious source of encouragement for this approach. This study, again, tries to address the usefulness of such approaches through some attention to how Nato has dealt with third-area conflicts over time.

Perhaps the most fundamentally important of all the political and military shifts which have occurred within the Alliance, from which a variety of specific disputes in turn have flowed, is the development of approximate economic equality between Europe and the United States. The days are past when the Europeans could be described as economic clients or dependents of the United States. This clearly was the case during the 1950s and most of the 1960s. Western Europe collectively has at times been able to establish somewhat more coherence in policy, reflecting in part the opportunity for greater independence from Washington. The European Community as a result enjoyed some limited success during the 1970s in developing a single co-ordinated voice on selected foreign-policy questions. This was sufficient to lead Henry Kissinger to complain in 1974 of a new challenge to American leadership and direction of the Alliance, implying at the same time that the Europeans' new unity made life difficult for the Americans, who no longer could so easily find cracks in the Community façade through which to widen the divisions between different national positions in Europe.

This general shift has been accompanied, rather predictably, by a series of specific policy disagreements between Europeans and Americans over the course of the past decade. These clashes have probably been most direct in relation to the complex, intense political rip tides of the Middle East. Increasing European economic capacity has provided both more opportunity for independence from Washington and a greater need than ever to try to ensure a reliable flow of essential petroleum. In the United States, a powerful emotional affinity for Israel has been reinforced by the domestic political influence of Jewish voters and pro-Israel organizations. Domestic production of approximately half the oil needed in the United States provided comparatively less opportunity for effective Arab political leverage. Western Europe, on the other hand, relies on Opec, and in particular proximate suppliers in the Middle East, for more than 80 per cent of oil needs. Hence the Europeans are much more susceptible to direct economic pressure from that source. Moreover, attitudes toward the opposing sides in the Middle East are fundamentally different from those of the Americans. The tie with Israel is not so strong, the domestic political calculus in West European nations different from in the United States, and certainly lingering sentimental ties to former colonial areas in the Arab world are stronger for Europeans than for Americans. The mix of interest and attitude is therefore very different from what determines policy in Washington.

Not surprisingly, therefore, clashes between Europe and the United States over Middle Eastern policy have occurred with some regularity in recent years. If none has been as wrenching as the Suez fiasco of 1956, they have been more threatening to the superpower simply because the United States no longer enjoys the dominant position of earlier years. During the 1973 Yom Kippur war in the Middle East, there were problems in securing British and West German co-operation in American resupply efforts for Israel. More recently, and also in many ways more significantly, there were difficulties associated with the European Community's own initiative toward the Middle East, an effort encouraged by the apparent dissipation of momentum in the Camp David peace process following the initial Egyptian–Israeli accord brokered by President Carter.

At the economic summit in Venice in June 1980, the European nations confronted the Americans – and Israel – with related demands to provide the Palestine Liberation Organization with official recognition as a party to negotiations in the region and remove reference to the Palestinians as 'refugees' from United Nations Security Council

Resolution 242, which addresses with emphasis the need for peace. Great Britain, which had abstained from and opposed these sorts of initiative in the past, joined in support of this one. Commentary in *Newsweek* magazine at the time underscored the negative consequences of the disagreement for Alliance affairs: 'The U.S. and Israel reply that the Europeans are simply caving in to oil blackmail. Neither side shows much inclination to budge. So all the signals are now set for another destructive storm in the Atlantic alliance.'[1]

Differences over the best manner to try to reconcile the dispute between Israel and the Arabs – step-by-step or comprehensive settlement, recognition of the P.L.O. first or only after acceptance of Israel – were further complicated by the renewed security attention devoted to the Middle East in general and the Persian Gulf area in particular. The large-scale exercise carried out by the 82nd Airborne Division in the region in 1981 dramatized most effectively the strong involvement of American national security interests in the Gulf region. The area has always been a source of considerable concern to Washington, with the commitment to Israel mixed with worry about Soviet expansionism and the inherent instability of a number of Arab states. The need to deal with various former – and current – European colonial powers regarding this part of the world, interchange that was perhaps most painful during the Suez crisis of 1956, has only brought home the capacity of events there to make mischief for relations among Atlantic-area nations.

The Opec price and supply initiatives of the early 1970s built upon this concern and anxiety, and transformed general fears about political instability and Soviet beach-heads into very concrete worries that vital oil supplies could be cut off rather easily. As the United States sought to extricate itself from military involvement in Indochina in the early 1970s, there was a natural attraction of attention to the Middle East. The U.S. Army began to focus future planning on problems of operation in desert environments. This was followed by the Carter Administration's efforts to establish a 'Rapid Deployment Force', which, despite being the target of much criticism, represented a concrete effort to address conventional military power projection challenges, especially but not exclusively in the Persian Gulf area. While the force might be discussed formally as designed to operate with maximum flexibility, the practical reality was that planning was directed mainly to Middle Eastern contingencies.

The Rapid Deployment Force represents one specific military

initiative, but opens the door to the wider subject of the appropriate role of the Atlantic Alliance in third-area conflicts today. There has in recent years been increasing discussion and debate over this matter. Again, this has occurred mainly in response to the focusing of the allies' attention on the Middle East and South-west Asia, and the questions this has raised about policy co-ordination. Should there be formal planning within the Alliance to deal with contingencies beyond a direct, overt Soviet invasion of Western Europe? Does the security of Western Europe require institutional readiness on the part of Nato to strike in the Middle East? Does the Alliance run the risk of blurring basic purposes through distraction into third areas? Elaboration on such questions in a more than rhetorical manner is one major goal of this study.

Although the growing importance of the Middle East to Western security has increased tensions between the United States and European partners, there is another, somewhat competitive, point which should be underlined at the outset – namely, that the Atlantic Alliance has never really been free of major policy problems and disagreements. The economic balance between the United States and Western Europe has tilted toward the latter, thus righting an imbalance resulting from the Second World War, but this has not created a situation which is either entirely new or unprecedented.

Meg Greenfield, a perceptive journalist who has analysed U.S. politics and foreign policy for a number of years, wrote in the spring of 1980, 'I have been trying to think of a time when the Alliance was in array.' She goes on to point out that correspondents and others more directly engaged in the foreign-policy process have consistently lamented the problems attending co-operation and the development of harmony in the Atlantic Alliance. She quotes Henry Kissinger in 1963, criticizing the Kennedy Administration for stirring up uneasiness and scepticism among the Europeans concerning American policies on security and decolonization. She concludes,

> Former Under Secretary of State George Ball was high up in the Administration Kissinger was criticising. But Kissinger was to be the central figure in administrations George Ball would tax with the same failures. And both, as now, would say the same, or worse, about another Administration – just as you can be sure that if either is back in office next year, he will be bombarded with similar charges.

Because she has a good sense of recent history, she is able to be fairly specific about earlier failings and disputes:

> John Kennedy's cancellation of the Skybolt missile – penciled in by the British as a prospective defense mainstay – created one of the more notable transoceanic uproars. So did some of his anti-colonial moves and so did what many Europeans regarded as a fixation with Cuba. Read Cuba for Iran. But the grandaddy, in every sense, of alliance disarray was surely Suez. . . .[2]

This bears directly on the principal objective of this study, which is not only to describe events involving Nato, but also to put contemporary difficulties and challenges into the proper historical context. Current problems are serious, to be sure, but not necessarily more serious than earlier problems and surely not of an entirely different order of magnitude. In this sense, the tone here is encouraging rather than discouraging.

2 Nato: The Ancient Alliance

The North Atlantic Treaty Organization is both one of the longest-lasting regional security alliances in history, and one of the most important and visible factors in current U.S. foreign policy. This in turn provides continuing insight into the paradoxes, tensions and ironies of the relationships involved. The pact is now almost forty years old. Arguably, however, the principal problems animating Alliance relations have changed very little over the past three decades. The overall strategic balance between the two superpowers, the United States and the Soviet Union, may have shifted – at least in sheer military terms – from favouring the former to favouring the latter; the relationships between different Atlantic-area states and the rest of the international system may have changed in various ways; and there has clearly been a diminution in the political influence of Washington on European capitals. This in turn is connected to the shifting economic relations among the Allies as the American hegemony has waned.

None the less, the Alliance in important respects has not changed that much since the early years in terms of basic policy issues dividing the parties involved. In various ways, the past had the same sort of overall political form as the present has. Recently there has been a renewal of strong debate within the United States over whether or not the Europeans are doing their share in terms of military contributions to the partnership. But this subject has also been a source of tension and debate from the very beginning. Why, asked the senior leadership of the Eisenhower Administration, are the Europeans so uncomfortable with the doctrine of massive retaliation? For members of the Truman Administration, the important national security report N.S.C.-68 – the linchpin of the new superpower's efforts in the defence field – had underscored a commitment to conventional strength and encouraged irritation with Nato partners unwilling to make equal sacrifices. The Lisbon conference in the early 1950s had made explicit that Nato would greatly increase conventional strength, thus providing a concrete reference point for military advocates who felt strongly that the pact was not meeting force goals and that this was not acceptable. For the American side, the main problem with this approach was that the Eisenhower Administration was from the beginning clearly committed to reducing emphasis on sizable conventional forces through concentration on the U.S. nuclear arsenal.

The American nuclear guarantee, raised to the status of principal component of security policy, did little to reassure insecure Europeans. Washington had gone from high pressure to do more in the conventional arena to the risk that attended threatening to make any armed conflict a nuclear one. The Europeans' dilemma was not the threat of particular American military policies; the problem rather was that a dependency relationship made them painfully aware that in strategic policy Washington was the actor and the various European capitals were essentially reactors.

To expand this point, focusing on the contemporary tensions and strains within Nato tends to mask the fundamental success of the institution, the importance of earlier disagreements and the simple fact that Nato has managed to survive as a political entity of consequence for more than three decades. Any realistic analysis of the problems now besetting the Alliance requires placing them in the wider historical context of what went before. This is particularly true for Nato, a political as well as a security association, and one which represents a significant influence on the relations among the Western allies and between them and the Eastern bloc. Current problems are in important respects similar to and different from those of earlier years. Serious disagreements have occurred throughout the life of the Alliance. The key for evaluation is recognition of the resilience of policies and institutions in overcoming barriers and achieving reconciliation among different viewpoints.

POST-WAR MILIEU

Nato was established in the difficult aftermath of the Second World War as a mechanism directly designed to contain the Soviet Union, and the organization clearly represents both the threat and the promise perceived by the framers. The Soviet threat was conceived explicitly to include ambitions to dominate the western half of Europe as well as the eastern. The large, ominous military shadow cast by the Red Army gave form to these fears. The disillusionments accompanying the period right after the war seemed to justify the belief that the other superpower was irreconcilably hostile as well as geographically ambitious *vis-à-vis* the West. By the late 1940s, hopes for satisfactory political co-operation between the Soviet Union and the major Western allies had broken down. Indeed, even before the conclusion of the conflict with Germany there were indications that the end of the war probably also would end the effective incentives for alliance between West and East. Poland, which had sparked the fighting in Europe in 1939, also served to represent the basic difference of view between the emerging post-war superpowers. The Soviet Union's insistence on sympathetic regimes directly on its own borders clashed with American insistence on Western-style free and democratic elections. Western support for the exiled London Poles was directly undercut by Soviet installation of the Lublin Polish goverment, a puppet regime following in the wake of the Red Army in the liberation of that unhappy country.

Varying interpretations put on the Yalta agreements concerning Poland by the Soviets and the Western allies, and the different tactics advocated by Churchill and Roosevelt in trying to cope with the situation, were the main early indications of the emerging Cold War. The behaviour of Stalin and the Red Army in standing aloof during the Polish Warsaw uprising against German occupation troops in 1944 raised serious American and British objections. And, indeed, the Soviet Union was pursuing fundamentally different interests regarding Poland and, beyond that nation, Eastern Europe as a whole. Hans J. Morgenthau observed in this connection,

> The Yalta agreements . . . were an attempt, doomed to failure from the outset, to maintain a modicum of Western influence in the nations of Eastern Europe which the Red Army had conquered. That influence was to be maintained through the instrument of free democratic elections. Yet in the view of the fear and hatred with which most of Eastern Europe has traditionally reacted to the colossus from the East, free elections in Eastern Europe could be considered by the Soviet Union only as a weapon with which first to limit, and then to destroy, Soviet control.[1]

Early disillusionment focused on Poland was quickly reinforced by events elsewhere. In 1945 and 1946, the Soviet occupation of Azerbaidjan in northern Iran, involvement in the Greek Civil War and conquest of other East European states, including Bulgaria, Hungary and Romania, all served to increase the Western powers' suspicions and heighten tension between East and West. In 1947, the Americans and British merged their sectors of Germany in economic terms, and this was followed by a breakdown of talks for achievement of national unification. The following year, an explicitly Communist government was installed in Czechoslovakia, and the Czech leader Jan Masaryk died under questionable circumstances. The American response was clear in terms of increasing international engagement to resist the Soviet Union, especially but not exclusively in Europe.[2] In 1947 also, President Truman issued his famous Doctrine, affirming the willingness of the United States to defend other nations, not just in Europe but anywhere. The threat of Soviet imperialism was not explicitly defined, but was clearly seen to be universal.

A much more positive related point is that the United States was undertaking a transformation of its traditional attitude toward the wider international system. There had of course been extensive debate within the country about the wisdom of direct involvement in the Second World War, but this had been resolved decisively in favour of intervention. This resolution was not the result of a naturally developed consensus, however, but rather was imposed by the Japanese military attack on Pearl Harbor. Yet, though the decision to enter the war was hardly taken dispassionately, once that course was selected there was no turning back, even after the conclusion of fighting with the Axis powers. A major psychological barrier had been crossed, in contrast to – and in part because of – the experience after the First World War. The entire thrust of informed opinion was for keeping the United States engaged in international politics, reflecting in part, no doubt, the influence of Roosevelt's effective, adroit wartime leadership, in part a desire to avoid repetition of the recognized mistakes of withdrawal into isolationism in the years following 1918.

A major factor in changing attitudes was the reality that the United States, even before the Second World War, had achieved major global economic influence, with extensive interests and concerns beyond its national borders. Although Britain had not yet been clearly supplanted as the world's principal industrial and commercial power, the trend toward decline was already apparent and the Americans were well within striking-distance of premier status. The last decades of the nineteenth century and the first of the twentieth provided growing statistical evidence that Britain was falling behind the United States and also Austria–Hungary, France, Germany and Russia in the rate of increase in production of key materials, including pig iron and ferro alloys, and steel ingots and castings. In the words of one perceptive observer, A. W. DePorte,

> The production of iron and steel are important yardsticks. French expenditures on armaments were overshadowed by Germany's, but how much wider the discrepancy in iron and steel production! By 1914 Great Britain was no longer the industrial leader of Europe. How startling it is to see that backward Russia, on the eve of World War 1, was already producing almost two-thirds as much steel as advanced Britain. In modern industry, as in defense expenditures, Germany was setting a new standard for power in Europe. But it was as overshadowed in industry by the United States (which in 1913 produced 32 million tons of steel) as in population by Russia.[3]

Economic growth was accompanied by expansion of military capabilities, even on the part of isolationist America, and a consequent uncertainty about the balance of power among the major nations.

The United States was engaged in hard-eyed evaluation of the new opportunities for national economic gain, specifically through penetrating the very large international British sphere of influence. Americans were ready to exploit their position of emerging economic primacy. The United States, while a close wartime ally of Britain, insisted in very businesslike fashion that accommodation be made to national economic interests. London's pound sterling was made convertible to U.S. dollars, and British markets were forced open to American goods. Washington was replacing London as the major Western international political capital; New York continued to replace London as the primary international commercial capital.

At the same time, conceptions about the best approach to the international system, including the international economic system, varied. On the one hand, the U.S. Treasury Department believed that universalism was best, Americans should not differentiate among regions of the globe, and that broad international institutions, such as the new United Nations structure, represented the best hope for the future. On the other hand, the State Department saw the world as a collection of nation states, argued that national security must be advanced through the security of individual states, and supported regional but not universal security pacts and related political institutions, or at least viewed the former with more enthusiasm that the latter.[4]

The role of personalities beyond President Roosevelt's, which has already been noted, should also be given appropriate attention. The senior leaders of the Truman Administration – including the President – played crucial roles, though not all of the same sort, in setting the course of policy. President Roosevelt may have set the basic trend toward post-war internationalism, but Truman and Secretaries of State George Marshall and Dean Acheson had actually to define and implement policy in more specific terms. Also to be noted in this regard are the senior Congressional leaders, especially Tom Connally and Arthur Vandenberg, respectively the most senior Democratic and Republican members on the Senate Foreign Relations Committee.

There is always a tendency to glamorize leading figures as events fade into the past, as long as those events are regarded in a positive or, better, heroic light. Policies seen as successful tend to enhance the status of those who are identified as responsible for them; there is a similar, inverse correlation in the case of failure. None the less, there is unusually strong testimony that the State Department was indeed very ably led during these years and consequently played an effective role in the negotiating process leading to the formation of Nato. One analyst has noted,

> For the first ten of the twelve months of [Nato treaty] negotiations, Marshall was Secretary of State and [Robert] Lovett, Under Secretary. Dean Rusk stated in 1976 that Lovett was Marshall's alter ego and that the 'combination of Marshall and Lovett as the leadership of the Department of State has never been equalled in our history and is not likely to be again.'

This is the voice of the conventional establishment, but the point stands after discounting for hyperbole. The Nato treaty also had formidable advocates at other senior levels of the bureaucracy, including two influential Soviet experts – Charles Bohlen, who was in charge of relations between the State Department and Congress, and George Kennan, who was Director of the State Department Policy Planning Staff. Somewhat lower down the ladder, John D. Hickerson, Director of the Office of European Affairs, and Theodore Achilles, Director of the Division of Western European Affairs, were also engaged in these initiatives. In effect, pro-Atlanticism was very heavily dominant in the upper echelons of the Department. Skill was important, but so was overall commitment to the same sort of post-war international structure, and here the Administration and the Department were well co-ordinated.[5]

Along with the important incentives which were encouraging the

United States toward a world role is the striking enthusiasm with which the new posture was assumed. There was a genuine sense of adventure in the attitude of many Americans, both in the population at large and among the leadership. Again, perhaps this reflects at least to some extent the exceptional ability of Roosevelt to inspire and energize the people. There was also the sense, long established, that the United States had a mission to spread democracy internationally, and this was enhanced by the perceived threat of the Soviet Union after the beginning of the Cold War period. Possibly another factor was that, with the settlement of the continental United States, there was a much greater willingness to look outward to the wider world. In any case, the shift in American attitudes, which was apparent during the war, well before the onset of the Cold War, is striking.

The transition from isolationist young nation, through major ally in the desperate struggle of the world war, to internationalist super-power was of course aided by the unusual dominance enjoyed by the United States in sheer economic terms. This involves not just the point, already mentioned, that British decline facilitated the emergence of the United States. Virtually all the other major industrial nations – Britain, France, Germany, Italy, Japan and the Soviet Union – were prostrate as a result of the devastation brought by the war. The first two decades after the end of the conflict meant that the American economy was of central, truly unprecedented importance. There are many inherent, special strengths of the American economic position, but the key element here was the absence of competition from other quarters. The much more difficult circumstances of more recent years have been a function of the return of the international system to the more customary situation of a number of competing centres of strength.

Finally, there is the point that Americans may have accepted the commitment represented by Nato more easily because they had, at least for a while, been able to rid themselves of major preoccupations elswhere, notably in Asia. That part of the world was the principal arena for the growth of American imperialism at the turn of the century – new relationships there contrasted with the familiar ones south of the border. This was the environment where expansion continued even after 'manifest destiny' had run out of territory in the continental United States, and was the region of the opponent which finally triggered American entry into the war – Japan.

Walter Lippmann, in perceptive fashion, got at this point in an article written for *Foreign Affairs* six and a half years before Pearl

Harbor. Not surprisingly for the time, he phrased his argument about the United States in the context of the Anglo-American great-power relationship:

> It may be that conditions are such that for the time being Britain must clarify her policy in Europe and America her policy in the Pacific. . . . this is to say that until Britain has settled the European question and feels secure in Europe, it will play no effective role in Asia, and until America has settled the Asiatic question and feels secure in the Pacific, it will play no effective part in Europe.[6]

The paradoxes and ironies inherent in American attitudes toward Asia and Europe are an important component in the total matrix of sentiment which guided U.S. foreign policy during the years immediately after the Second World War. Arguably, the United States has stronger emotional links with Asia even if cultural ties are stronger with Europe. Certainly the experience of three wars in the Pacific in less than five decades has reinforced a sense of involvement with Asia. The gradual but firm shift of U.S. trade from Europe to Asia provides very tangible evidence that the latter region may be overshadowing the former in the eyes of Washington.

For Europeans, the Nato agreement was desirable as an obvious, effective mechanism for bringing needed American security guarantees into being, and was congruent, moreover, with more longstanding attitudes toward the Soviet Union and, earlier, Russia. The treaty would secure American commitment to the defence of Western Europe and ensure that in future there would be no delays such as had occurred in 1914–17 and 1939–41 in obtaining the direct involvement of the large power on the other side of the Atlantic. Facing bleak economic prospects and the menacing military power of the Soviet Union, there was no longer room for Europeans to feel superior to the Americans or to pretend that they could defeat the large Eastern bloc in war without American assistance. To view the Soviets as threatening was not really a novelty after the end of the war, despite the alliance arrangements which had existed with major West European powers at the start of the First World War and after the German invasion of the Soviet Union in 1940. Paul Seabury has described the encompassing, historically rooted conflict in this manner:

> The conception of cold-war conflict as arising from an East–West configuration – while spatially ambiguous – stressed geography,

culture and history; contemporary ideological questions were only
manifestations of deeper historical tensions dividing 'two worlds'.
New conflict was thus rendered plausible when related to more
ancient European experience.[7]

Of course, ideological conflict between East and West would combine with older cultural and diplomatic differences to provide the
tapestry of Cold War conflict. To see the conflict in purely military,
doctrinal or contemporary strategic terms would be to oversimplify.
Seabury stresses this point in his analysis:

1947 was the year and point in time when all the analytic features of
the conflict suddenly were fused together. A 'mere' Soviet–
American struggle for power, stripped of all the other significances
and concerned 'merely' with matters, say, of national security and
national influence, would describe a conflict much different from
the immensely complex one which we have experienced since then.[8]

The danger of Marxism–Leninism was brought centre-stage by conservatives in the United States, and to some extent in Europe, as the
main threat to stability and freedom in the post-war world. This added
fervour and intensity to the conflict that would not otherwise have
been present. No doubt the ideological aspects of the struggle with
Germany and Japan facilitated a similar reading of the post-war environment. The reality of ideological conflict between the United
States and the Soviet Union, between a West that was mainly democratic and capitalist, and an Eastern bloc that was largely neither,
cannot be denied. Yet focusing on the ideological character of the
conflict underscored the gulf between the two sides, and rendered any
sort of accommodation far more difficult to achieve.

Essentially, then, the Atlantic Alliance was forged through a combination of different interests which were none the less congruent – a
necessary condition for the formation of political coalitions – and built
upon both sweeping ambitions and more concrete political goals.
There was a powerful overlay of ideology which lent intensity to the
whole set of proceedings. The United States was strongly motivated by
the conviction that it had to become directly involved in international
affairs, but there were also concrete economic interests fuelling the
directions of policy. Likewise, there were idealistic conceptions about
the promotion of international co-operation through collective
security arrangements as well as the new United Nations. But there

were also immediate fears about the encroachment of the Soviet Union on Western Europe.

Self-interest, especially in cold economic terms; regional interests, especially in seeing the political need for alliance with Western Europe; and at least the idea of broad humanitarian interest, in seeing Europe recover economically and remain or become democratic politically – these factors all contributed to the ultimate Nato treaty. The Americans also had the advantage of previous lack of involvement in European affairs. If the American style contrasts markedly with the British, the new superpower could at least work as honest broker among the Europeans. The United States had supported the victorious side in both world wars, and there were advantages in previous isolation. David N. Schwartz, in an inclusive review of Nato issues, notes for example that the United States 'is . . . distant enough from the intra-European quarrels of the past to be able to offer credible leadership to the other members of the alliance.'[9]

THE TREATY: PRELUDE, STRUCTURE, IMPACT

The final treaty combined these different incentives, implicitly reflecting the sweeping ambitions and explicitly addressing more concrete, immediate concerns. In one sense the document was ambiguous, with the formulators seeking to engage the United States in Europe and encourage broader political co-operation. In another, the treaty had very specific common defence purposes, strictly limited in geographic terms. The greatest ambitions were ultimately not achieved; the concrete goals ensured that the treaty would actually be relevant. Had the broadest ambitions been tied more explicitly to the document's prose, there is little doubt that the effort would have failed, at least over the longer term.

The setting-up of Nato followed a series of more limited security steps. These were the preliminary building-blocks on which the final structure was erected. Indirectly, of course, Article 51 of the United Nations Charter encouraged this sort of security relationship. More concretely, in March 1947 the British and French signed the Treaty of Dunkirk. The main potential threat noted at that time was Germany. The text of the treaty mentioned that the signing nations would protect one another from any threat, 'arising from the adoption by Germany of a policy of aggression, or from action by Germany designed to facilitate such a policy'. The treaty was clearly encouraged by the tensions which were growing between the Western nations and the Soviet Union. A year later, in March 1948, the Dunkirk alliance was widened into the Brussels Pact. The resulting Western Union, as the structure was titled, included Belgium, Britain, France, Luxembourg and the Netherlands.[10]

The British played an important role in effecting this marriage of European powers and, ultimately, in bringing in the United States as well. The Labour government's Foreign Secretary, Ernest Bevin, was apparently especially effective in dealing with Jean Monnet, soon to be universally described as the father of the European Community, in forging the European Coal and Steel Community, and, more widely, in dealing with the foreign-policy officials of the Truman Administration in forging the Atlantic Alliance. As in the past, Britain was acting as a vital catalyst among nations. As Lippmann would see it, the British had come to terms with their European concerns, and were using this success, albeit after bitter total war, to broker an attachment between the United States and Europe. It should be emphasized, however, that their interests were at this point defined solely in military security terms, which was not such a great departure in traditional stance. Economic co-operation among the continentals and Marshall Plan aid were all well and good; the movement of Britain into Europe in straightforward economic terms, as trade patterns changed, would be a much longer and more painful exercise.

These security accords were part of a larger tapestry that included a truly momentous aid programme, the Marshall Plan. This effort represented the most important component of a genuine revolution in American policy in political as well as economic terms. The plan, which was proposed initially in June 1947 by Secretary of State George Marshall, included American assistance to Europe amounting to $20,000 million, to be distributed over a period of five years. This extraordinary sum was devoted to the goal of providing a capital base sufficient to generate income at a level a full 25 per cent above pre-war levels. The Soviet bloc was invited to participate – indeed, only fascist Spain among European powers was excluded – but chose not to do so. A total of sixteen nations were involved in the effort, which formally got under way in June 1948. The Marshall Plan was a clear and very sharp reversal of previous American isolationism vis-à-vis Europe and European problems. Another key feature of the effort was a linkage of economic aid to political goals. Americans wanted European recovery partly for straightforward humanitarian purposes; the region after all had been thoroughly devastated by the war. There was also a desire to revive what was clearly a principal market area for the United States. Finally, there was the obvious goal of preventing Soviet encroachment into Western Europe.

It would be difficult to exaggerate the wrenching sense of frustration, disappointment and alarm which animated American attitudes toward the Soviet Union following wartime co-operation. While the United States was becoming bound to Europe through security and economic accords, the cleavage with the East in Europe was becoming sharper and deeper. In June 1948, the Soviets left the *Kommandatura*, the joint Allied council for the supervision of Berlin, and began a land and water blockade of the city. This in turn led to the Allied response of a major extended airlift to maintain the city. Encircled Berlin was effectively supplied through the air corridors, the one transportation medium not cut off. The frustrated Soviets ended their blockade in the late spring of the following year. This led directly to the Western decision to merge the British, French and U.S. zones of occupation into the single Federal Republic of Germany.

The Berlin blockade represented a fundamentally important event in the evolution of the Cold War. After the crisis, Germany was divided into two opposing parts, each under the direct control of one of the increasingly hostile superpowers. The 'Iron Curtain', as Churchill had described the division of Europe, was clearly visible as a single great dividing-line running from north to south across the continent, the focus of armed hostility between the two camps. Before the Berlin Crisis, there was still some hope of restoring a Europe of nation states with relations that were both fluid and changing. After the blockade, this hope no longer possessed credibility. The pre-war political map of Europe seemed to be gone for ever. In the United States, both the Democratic and the Republican leadership consistently supported the new international engagements and, especially, the new European security pacts. As early as the 1948 presidential campaign, this national stance was apparent, reflected, among other places, in the bipartisan Vandenberg Resolution of June, and the foreign-policy efforts of the Truman Administration played no significant role in the otherwise intense and divisive presidential contest with Dewey in that year.

These varied accords and challenges led rather naturally to the formation of Nato. The agreement, negotiated by Secretary of State Marshall and, after he developed health problems, Dean Acheson, was ratified by the Senate on 21 July 1949. The key elements were Article 5, which declared that an attack on one would be considered an attack on all, and Article 6, which set clear territorial limits to the treaty. The new security treaty was systematically sold to leading foreign-policy figures in the United States in a way reflecting the high importance placed on the initiative by the Administration in Washington. The period March to June 1949 was devoted to a major public-relations exercise in an effort to convince American foreign-policy opinion of the desirability of the treaty. George Kennan, who generally disliked the automatic character of many treaties, was persuaded to support this one and do so publicly.[11]

Nato was from the start designed to be a comprehensive organization in terms of framework. A complex bureaucratic structure was established. While the goals of the Alliance were straightforward and relatively simple, the mechanisms set up to implement them were complicated. Reflecting the fact that this was inherently a political as well as a military organization, there was a need to reconcile a considerable range of national interests and inherently conflicting goals. The Nato structure, partly as a result of this state of affairs, had three separate commands. Because the United States and Great Britain had concluded the war as the dominant nations in the West, they were naturally the principal powers in the Alliance structure, and this earlier reality continues to be reflected in formal terms. The Supreme Allied Commander Europe, based at Shape (Supreme Headquarters Allied Powers Europe), is in charge in continental Europe. By custom, this senior general has been an American and also the commander of the U.S. European Command. There is also a chief of the Atlantic naval area, Aclant, who is a U.S. admiral, as well as a head of the English Channel Area, Acchan, who has for understandable reasons been a British admiral. Thus has the bureaucratic formality reflected an increasingly outdated political reality.

In addition to the three basic military commands, there is a bureaucratic structure at Casteau, near Brussels, in Belgium. This is the administrative nerve centre of the Alliance, complete with large staffs, complex committees, and other paraphernalia reflecting not so much the dominant power centres in national terms as the constellation of interests that had to be reconciled initially, and still have to be addressed, for the partnership to function. This organizational structure has displayed many of the features which in broader political terms have characterized the practical daily relations among the nations involved – i.e. a large number of complicated institutions which often do not mesh well; a constant need for compromise and reconciliation of interests; the dangers of inertia and complacency; and, most serious of all over the long term, the danger that Alliance structures might become ends in themselves, especially for those involved in staffing them. Perhaps especially in a military alliance, there is a constant need to measure readiness and to beware of the temptations toward unthinking acceptance of the *status quo* that are characteristic of all large organizations.

The Korean War provided a major further shock to the nervous system of the emerging Western Alliance. The invasion of South Korea by the North in late June 1950 immediately involved U.S. military forces along with those of fifteen United Nations members, and soon included the mainland Chinese as well. The war was instructive regarding developing Atlantic-area relationships in several respects. First, and most profoundly, the war immediately was interpreted by American leaders in terms of the dangers and importance of Atlantic-area relations. This was at least part of the motivation for General Omar N. Bradley's statement in Congressional hearings that the Joint Chiefs of Staff would not support an expansion of the conflict, because 'this strategy would have involved us in the wrong war, at the wrong place, at the wrong time, and with the wrong enemy'.[12] Just as twenty years later President Kennedy and his advisers felt that somehow Soviet missiles in Cuba were related to a thrust on Berlin, so in the Korean War period there was a constant preoccupation with Soviet motives toward Europe.

Second, in the United States the war in Korea contributed directly to a sense of betrayal and internal Communist menace that would be exploited in the arena of domestic politics, and not just by Senator Joseph McCarthy. Secretary of State Dean Acheson had in effect declared publicly that Formosa (Taiwan) as well as Korea were outside the Pacific defence boundaries of the United States. The Secretary understandably disagreed that his words had given any direct encouragement to the North Koreans, noting among other statements on the subject in his memoirs,

Later it was argued that my speech 'gave the green light' to the attack on South Korea by not including it within the 'defense perimeter'. This was specious, for Australia and New Zealand were not included either, and the first of all our mutual defense agreements was made with Korea. If the Russians were watching the United States for signs of our intentions in the Far East, they would have been more impressed by the two years agitation for withdrawal of combat forces from Korea, the defeat in Congress of a minor aid bill for it, and the increasing discussion of a peace treaty with Japan.[13]

The more significant point does not relate to Acheson's anti-Communism, which can hardly be in doubt, despite some of the political accusations of the time, but rather to the intense fear of the Soviet Union and Soviet Communism, which led critics to seize on his speech as a means to criticize him and, through him, the Truman Administration. There is also the fact that the Secretary was very much a part of the Anglophile American foreign-policy establishment of the time, which may well have contributed to a tendency to slight Asian complexities, at least on occasion, in favour of a focus on Europe and the wider Atlantic area.

Third, the Korean War, because of the two other considerations just described, permitted – indeed compelled – a major American military build-up and brought about European rearmament as well. Any debate remaining in the United States about the need to have military muscle behind new international involvement was closed off. The Americans took the opportunity to raise the specific matter of West German military rearmament, which the French understandably deflected. They proposed a European Defence Community which would involve German components but not under direct German national control.

The challenge represented by the Korean War also led directly to the Lisbon force goals for Nato. Meeting in Portugal in early 1952, the Nato Council agreed to a plan to increase very substantially the military levels of the Alliance. It was decided that within a year military capacity should be increased to fifty divisions and 4000 aircraft, with 'strong' naval forces. This reflected not just the reaction to armed conflict in Asia but also fears of a Soviet bloc believed to be very heavily armed in conventional military terms. Again, the shadow of the Red Army was quite significant for the course of Atlantic-area foreign policy. Unfortunately, Nato was never able fully to implement these plans. The beginnings of armistice talks in Korea reduced already inadequate incentives to continue with the armament efforts.[14] Hence, the Lisbon goals stood primarily as a reminder not of Nato determination in the face of a perceived Soviet challenge, but rather of the very serious problems involved in trying to increase national contributions to the regional security pact.

Overall, the 1950s was not a period when the Americans, or even the Europeans, felt particularly secure from attack. Quite the reverse in fact: the decade, especially the first part, was a time of intense security concern in both military and political terms. In the military dimension, having a nuclear monopoly or clear dominance did not provide reassurance in confronting a Soviet Union which was viewed as expanding territorially in virtually every direction, east and west, where it was not clearly opposed. Western leaders even at that time were more impressed by the limits imposed by the enormous destructive power at their disposal than by the leverage this might provide with the Soviet Union. The point is not that the Americans refrained from forms of 'atomic diplomacy' *vis-à-vis* the Soviet Union, using the threat of atomic weapons to pursue political goals. Indeed, Dulles in particular was notable for threatening to use the bomb, and throughout the decade massive retaliation was formal U.S. strategic doctrine. Rather, the point is that this approach to policy was fully congruent with, and no doubt spurred by, Western perceptions of being on the defensive against the Soviets.

In recent years, in the face of the very grave problems besetting the Atlantic Alliance, there has been a tendency to look back on the 1950s as an almost ideal time in terms of Alliance relations. This reflects more than anything the great turmoil and strain we face today rather than any genuine tranquillity in earlier years. The Eisenhower years in fact witnessed some of the most severe trials in the history of Nato. If Nato seemed a more stable alliance then – and in some respects it was – the answer lies more in the economic and military characteristics of U.S.– European and U.S.–Soviet relations than in anything else. The Alliance at least had the reassurance of a rather predictable political environment, one less fluid, but also for that reason less malleable, than the situation in the 1970s and 1980s.

First, there was the basic fact of life of American economic dominance. The United States at the conclusion of the Second World War had by far the strongest and most prosperous economic system in the world. The Americans had an economic strength *vis-à-vis* other nations which had not been seen before – even at the height of the British Empire – and perhaps will not be witnessed again. There were a multitude of benefits as a result, not only for Americans but also for the many nations that came under the American economic penumbra. The Bretton Woods system guaranteed that there would be fundamental monetary stability, from which would develop fundamental stability in trade patterns, at least until the end of the 1950s. The dollar was pegged explicitly to gold, with a value reinforced besides through the strength of the American economy. Other currencies were pegged against the dollar, giving security and stability to the entire international financial market.

The system depended directly on the reliability of the linchpin dollar, but for most of the Cold War period the dollar value was very stable; there was no pressure against the $35 per ounce gold price. Likewise, the American economy penetrated and dominated those of the other main industrial nations. Even those which were beginning to make some progress competing with the Americans, including penetration of the domestic U.S. market, did not provide any sort of broad threat. American economic resources were simply too vast; the rest of the industrial world was still struggling to recover from the effects of the world war. Indeed, the American economy was so strong that the U.S. government could even protect the still-rebuilding industries of Japan and Europe with preferential trading-arrangements and tolerate restrictive practices.

Second, the United States enjoyed at least until the middle of the 1950s a very decisive nuclear military edge over the Soviets. The capacity of U.S. B-47 and, later, B-52 bombers to devastate the Soviet Union led directly to U.S. strategic dominance. Until the middle of the 1950s, the Soviet Union did not have a similar capacity. The *de facto* nuclear monopoly effectively neutralized the enormous conventional military strength of the Red Army. In a sense, American economic strength provided the stage upon which political conflicts were to be played out, and American nuclear capacity provided a primary tool with which to influence international politics. As a result, the United States for the first time not only was engaged heavily and broadly in the wider world of foreign affairs, but also exercised that role as a monopolist in nuclear military power. The nation was for a crucial initial period in the nuclear age not one of two roughly equal military nuclear superpowers; rather, the United States was the single dominant international power in both economic and military terms.

The main problem for the United States was that neither perceptions nor political reality correlated exactly with this very great strength. Americans felt themselves beset by threatening national-security demons, and in fact having great military destructive capacity did not translate directly into cost-free imposition of political will. The early 1950s were after all the years when Senator McCarthy was at the height of his influence and internal political subversion was a governmental preoccupation of pervasive importance. We are well advised to remember that President Truman, not a conservative Republican, was the one who instituted a programme of loyalty oaths and security checks. The domestic witch hunts demonstrated a growing fear of the political threat represented by Communism, in turn tied to the influence of the Soviet Union.

Also, exertions of American influence were hardly decisive or overwhelming. The Korean War was concluded after a threat to use nuclear weapons, but only following a costly, debilitating three-year conventional conflict. The threat was not effectively repeated elsewhere, despite the emphasis of Secretary of State Dulles on massive retaliation as the main approach to national military–political strategy. The stress on possible first use of nuclear weapons was largely theoretical, or perhaps (given the attitudes and style of the Secretary) theological, rather than practical. The Korean precedent, if that is an apt description, was not followed elsewhere. In Indochina, most dramatically, the Administration was, to be sure, divided in opinion concerning the most appropriate response to the French defeat at Dien Bien Phu, but Eisenhower ultimately prevailed and neither nuclear nor direct conventional military involvement was undertaken. North Vietnam was conquered by Ho Chi Minh's Viet Minh forces and the French were defeated while the United States stood by.

More directly related to this analysis, European affairs were not dramatically changed because of the U.S. nuclear monopoly. There were no overt, aggressive moves on the part of the West to change the *status quo* in the East, despite the fact that Poland's domination by the Soviets was seen as contradicting the main goal of the allies in the Second World War in Europe. Nor was there an effective move to change the reality that Berlin was a source of constant friction and occasional crisis. Again, there were rhetorical initiatives by the Eisenhower Administration urging 'liberation' of Eastern Europe, carrying over from the excesses of the 1952 presidential campaign. When crisis opportunities arose, of the sort that might have provided excuses for direct military initiative, the Administration was in fact quite cautious. The armed revolt in Hungary in 1956, encouraged in part by American propaganda broadcasts, and the protests in Poland during the same year, found the Eisenhower Administration unwilling to provide any direct aid to the insurgents. The changes which did occur in the territory controlled by the East – in particular, the movement of Austria from the Communist bloc to a neutral stance in 1955 – had little to do with American nuclear dominance or military threats of any kind, explicit or implicit.

Indeed, the latter part of the decade witnessed some severe diplomatic setbacks for the notion of Atlantic Alliance unity, even considering the importance of the American military and economic factors. These included the victory of Castro's revolution in Cuba, the renewed Berlin crisis, the highly belligerent rhetoric of the Soviet leader Nikita Khrushchev, the successful testing of Soviet ballistic missiles and the perception – closely related to the nuclear one – of the large, growing Soviet military threat to the United States.

SUEZ AND AFTER

The most severe reversal for the Eisenhower Administration and the wider Alliance occurred in the Middle East. The Suez crisis shook the Nato structure to its foundations, and this fact was less apparent only because the dominance of the United States masked the fissures. None the less, the reverberations from Suez continued for years, both challenging and limiting the capacity of Nato nations to co-operate. The crisis took place in the context of uneasy relations betwen Eisenhower and Dulles, on the one hand, and British Prime Minister Anthony Eden, on the other. There was simply a personality clash between the direct Americans and the aristocratic Englishman, complicated by the fact that Eden was feeling considerable pressure from the right wing of his own Conservative party to be more forceful in addressing developments in the Middle East. Perhaps the British, French and Israelis were encouraged in their surprise invasion of the Sinai Peninsula and seizure of the Suez Canal by Dulles's intransigence concerning negotiations with Egyptian leader Nasser. Yet the American Secretary of State apparently was rigid for reasons which had little to do with the Egyptian regime: he was, as usual, focusing very directly on the dangers represented by the Soviet Union.[15]

The extent of the miscalculations by the Europeans and the Israelis was quite evident in Eisenhower's angry reaction to the surprise: 'All right, Foster, you tell 'em that, goddam it, we're going to do everything that there is so we can stop this thing.'[16] The President's remark was immediately in reaction to the Israeli invasion. Unfolding events showed that the British and French were also heavily involved, to such an extent that they vetoed a U.S. resolution entered in the U.N. Security Council, demanding Israeli withdrawal.[17]

Eisenhower immediately mobilized the considerable resources of the U.S. government for the effort to stymie the invasion. Telling leverage was applied to the British. Treasury Secretary George Humphrey, on Eisenhower's express instructions, refused to allow a draw-down on U.S. dollars from the International Monetary Fund to support the British pound, then falling in the markets as a result of the developing war. Chancellor of the Exchequer Harold Macmillan, a supporter of the Suez adventure, quickly changed his own position. The rest of the Eden government followed suit. The French government of Premier Guy Mollet, dependent on British logistical support, and subject to American pressures, also agreed to halt military operations.[18]

The British moved effectively, and overall rather expeditiously, to counteract the negative effects of the Suez fiasco. The operation had been conceived and carried out in the utmost secrecy, resulting in suspicion and division within the usually solid ranks of the British diplomatic service and the government. The debate in the House of Commons on the matter really cannot be so described: the reaction was rather a raucous, outraged protest from the Opposition that made genuine interchange impossible. In the final result, neither the old-fashioned imperialists nor the anti-imperial left had their positions vindicated. Britain could still try such a manoeuvre, so out of place in the world of emerging anti-colonial nationalism combined with economic vulnerability, yet could not succeed without American support.

In the face of these great problems, Macmillan as the new Prime Minister acted quickly to establish better relations with Washington. He was far more skilful than Eden in handling both Eisenhower and Dulles. In concrete terms, he was able to secure amendment of the McMahon Act in the United States to permit sharing of nuclear information with Britain. He also acquired verbal agreement from President Eisenhower to share the new Skybolt nuclear missile, a development which would lead to problems during the Kennedy Administration but seemed a most promising step toward reconciliation as Eisenhower's tenure moved toward its conclusion. If Suez was a disaster, it was not an unmitigated one: at least the contemporary limits on British power were demonstrated. Macmillan, and the British, were never again to forget the fundamental lesson of dependence on American economic as well as military power in basic political terms.

The second half of the 1950s, while bringing about a demonstration of the weakness of London and Paris in direct confrontation with Washington, also showed the emergence of West Germany as a major political actor. The burden of war guilt, clearly assigned and deserved – in contrast to the situation after the First World War – plus the lack of clarity regarding national burdens, made the German role especially challenging. In 1954, in the wake of a highly emotional debate, the French National Assembly voted down the proposition for a European

Defence Community, in large part because of the inclusion of the Federal Republic as a partner in the enterprise. Yet in 1955 the Federal Republic gained admission to Nato as an equal partner. Thus the skilled manoeuvring and rhetoric of Chancellor Konrad Adenauer achieved the key victory of acceptance as an equal among the Western allies.

One perceptive analyst of the important transition to legitimacy wrote:

On May 9, 1955, the Federal Republic of Germany formally became the fifteenth member of the North Atlantic Treaty Organization. From the viewpoint of most Western observers, the major problem surrounding a German contribution to Western defence had now been resolved. There still was some popular German opposition to rearmament, focused primarily on the moral issues involved and the consequences for future reunification. But the results of the 1953 elections had vindicated the chancellor's decision to rearm and had given him the parliamentary strength needed to proceed. It now seemed only a question of time until the long-sought and long-promised 500,000-man German forces were ready. . . . It was not to be that easy.[19]

Eisenhower's second term opened with – indeed, was preceded by – a shift in American military policy and strategy. This did not represent a fundamental change in direction but instead increased emphasis on economy in manpower and reliance on massive air power to deter war. The New Look policy of massive retaliation, stressed by the Eisenhower Administration soon after taking office, was reinvigorated and in more extreme form. The *New York Times* in mid-July 1957 reported that Admiral Arthur Radford, chairman of the U.S. Joint Chiefs of Staff, had supervised an analysis which concluded in favour of cuts of up to 800,000 men from the nation's military forces by the end of the decade.[20]

The twin incentives paramount in the minds of the Radford group were economic necessity, in keeping with the President's worries about the negative effects of military spending, and technological advance, in line with the continuing popular belief that machines, at least of a certain level of complexity, could replace men in military missions. The Army was the focus of the heaviest planned reductions – 450,000 men if the programme was in fact carried out. This in turn meant that the American military presence in other countries would be reduced. The Eisenhower Administration denied press reports about plans for military cuts, but the immediate political and diplomatic reaction was very sharp and the issue fuelled the domestic political debate through the 1960 presidential campaign, both directly and indirectly.[21]

The Radford debate brought an especially strong negative reaction from West Germany, for understandable reasons. The American military presence there was quite substantial, so that in turn was where a large percentage of the proposed cuts would have to occur. West Germany remained in the front line of confrontation with the Soviet bloc. Adenauer went through various obvious moves to indicate displeasure and protest, including recall of ambassadors for consultation. His situation was naturally complicated by the German military rearmament underway. He appealed to Dulles, as always a good friend of the West German leader and regime, and was successful. Dulles apparently favoured the Radford Plan, but favoured Adenauer more, and they in turn were able to carry the day with the President. This demonstrated not only the influence of the West German leader: the Federal Republic had finally arrived as an ally equal among others, whose support and opposition would carry considerable weight in policy decisions by the partners.

DE GAULLE

If the second half of the 1950s brought retreat for Britain and revival for West Germany, the period was one of profound turmoil and change for France. Of the three main West European powers, France was arguably throughout the decade the least stable politically. The Federal Republic emerged steadily as a national entity under the continuing forceful leadership of Adenauer. Britain's historic foundation was falling away, but the nation did not take too much notice, despite the harsh lesson of Suez. Only France suffered a series of shocks to the political nervous system which precluded either adjustment on the British model or growth of capacity in a manner similar to the Germans.

The greatest single trauma of the post-war period for the French was the defeat at Dien Bien Phu, and the consequent surrender of the northern part of Vietnam to the Viet Minh forces. The trauma of disaster in the colonial wars reverberated through the domestic political system, diminishing what was left of national self-confidence during this period. Frustration abroad was mirrored in instability at home, as a series of national governments attempted without success to construct policy consensus and stability. Revolving-door cabinets, inability to govern among the drastically conflicting political cultures of France, and the general perception of weakness at home and abroad all contributed to the reality of the notion of the sick man of post-war Western Europe.

Even before de Gaulle returned to power as head of government, the French were showing signs of increasing restlessness within Nato. While Britain in 1957 moved clearly toward greater rapport with Washington, France travelled in the opposite direction. The French set large, and finally unacceptable, conditions for deployment of IRBMs – intermediate-range ballistic missiles – on their soil. They wanted not only a dual-key arrangement for launching missiles, similar to that won by the British, but also U.S. technical and financial assistance for production of their own force. The Americans would not agree to this, and the French must have understood from the start what the character of Washington's response would be.

De Gaulle, when requested, moved into this situation to take charge once again as head of government. For various reasons, he was ideal for the role. He personified various traditions in the polity, as different analysts have pointed out: he was obviously monarchical in style, the use of referenda was in tune with radical populism, and his military record and the political tools he employed carried a whiff of Napoleon. General de Gaulle, brought back to national leadership to retain Algeria in the colonial fold, demonstrated ruthlessness by abruptly changing course, abandoning the conservative officers who had returned him to power, and cutting the nation's losses in that part of the world. If the imagery of influence and confidence – and a sense of history – could help decisively to restore the nation's self-confidence, reduction of commitments and frustrating involvements abroad could provide room for manoeuvre and useful resources on the European stage.

One of President de Gaulle's other early moves was to propose in 1958 a three-power directorate of Nato. France, Britain and the United States would effectively control nuclear weapons and wider Alliance decision-making. The President made the basic approach to the other two allies by means of formal letters. He was irritated that, at least from his perspective, no clear response was forthcoming from either. There are a number of fascinating possible turning-points in the relationship between France and the other Nato nations, especially the

United States, during de Gaulle's years of leadership and increasing independence from the rest of the Alliance. Surely this one is a particularly interesting source of speculation about what might have been.

While moving to secure his domestic power base – among other measures, by constitution – de Gaulle also became active more widely in European and Atlantic-area diplomacy, going well beyond nuclear-forces matters. We tend to forget now that he initially did not cast himself in the role of enemy of Washington's involvement in Europe or closer co-operation among the major powers in the Alliance, a point demonstrated well by his nuclear-directorate scheme. From the beginning, however, he did make clear that his foreign-policy conceptions involved nation states as not only the pre-eminent but virtually the only international actors. Notions of an emerging supranational entity in Western Europe, to say nothing of the vaguely defined independent Atlantic community, had no place in his world view. In retrospect, perhaps his strongest claim to both a sense of history and accurate prediction of the future revolves around this appreciation of the primary importance and durability of the state in the face of much more visionary schemes for organizing the Atlantic area. At the same time, one of his first initiatives after taking power was to propose that a directorate of the three nuclear Nato partners be established. Certainly, as the British moved closer to a decision to try to enter the Common Market, the memory of their casual, if not cavalier, treatment of the French leader's suggestion was a major disadvantage.

De Gaulle also moved in other directions, in a manner which was not inconsistent but designed to establish France as a separate actor, one capable of setting up a variety of different lines with various governments. There was an early, highly successful meeting with Konrad Adenauer of West Germany. In a theme which would recur in Franco-German relations in the years to follow, the two old national adversaries found that they had more than a little a common in a world in which Europe was deeply shadowed by the arsenals of the two superpowers. Indeed, perhaps de Gaulle's greatest accomplishment in Europe was his ability to stimulate *rapprochement* with the nation which aroused such bitter memories as well as strong negative contemporary sentiments among so many of his countrymen.

In sum, the French President was able to act clearly, often quickly, frequently in subtle ways, and in total established both his secure domestic power base, which survived the most extreme efforts by assassins to remove him, and a distinctive foreign-policy posture. This was done in the context of a troubled, divided political culture at home and following on a long series of very weak governments. His ultimate achievement was to forge that divided culture into singular, legitimate national political institutions. Consequently, his accomplishments in office must be counted as among the most impressive, and certainly the most dramatic, of any of the post-war national leaders of the Atlantic area.

Meanwhile, as both the 1950s and the Eisenhower Administration drew to a close, American policy and political debate continued to be occupied with the dilemmas of not only the Atlantic Alliance but also a range of other security commitments around the globe which had been energetically constructed by the anti-Communist Secretary of State, John Foster Dulles. This global effort to ring the Soviet Union with bilateral and regional security pacts, to replicate Nato again and again in different geographic locations and forms, did not prevent the development of attitudes in the United States, especially among informed people, that the nation was losing the race for military strength and political influence to the Soviets. The Eisenhower years brought economic growth, low inflation and absence of war. The President himself was enormously popular personally, as much because he effectively symbolized national virtue and ideals as for any specific qualities of leadership or decisions taken. Yet there was, especially among Democrats and members of the intelligentsia – but by no means these groups exclusively – the feeling that something was missing in both the tone and the direction of government policy. This included domestic as well as foreign policy. The Rockefeller Brothers Fund supported a series of major, well-publicized policy reports that were highly critical of the *status quo*. These in turn became important elements in Senator John Kennedy's successful campaign for the presidency as well as Governor Nelson Rockefeller's unsuccessful challenge to Vice-President Richard Nixon for the Republican nomination in 1960.

THE 1960 CAMPAIGN

There were four topics in particular which seemed to hurt the Eisenhower Administration in the way they developed in both the international system and the domestic political arena: the nebulous but important concept of leadership; the Soviet Union's alleged superiority in missiles and related worries about the balance of forces between Nato and the Warsaw Pact; the crisis over West Berlin; and the tensions with, and debate over what to do about, the Castro regime in

Cuba. On the leadership question, Eisenhower's health problems grew more serious during his second term, fuelling criticism that the President was not fully up to the job, while the emergence of Nikita Khrushchev as the Soviet leader fully in charge provided a challenger who was, to say the least, dynamic, energetic and threatening. In the duel for psychological advantage, and a stronger image, the United States seemed to come off second best.

Closely associated with the aggressive Soviet stance and American worry about international ineffectiveness was the missile-gap issue. Khrushchev's belligerent style and threatening stance, his constant threats to unleash nuclear war and his continuation of nuclear tests in the atmosphere served almost relentlessly to focus attention on the arms race and possible general war. Informed U.S. opinion increasingly was persuaded that the country was falling behind the Soviets in the missile race. This in turn brought the subject to the very centre of the stage in the unfolding campaign for the presidential nomination and the presidency in 1960.

The Eisenhower Administration held to the position that the nation's security position was quite strong, but at the same time there were efforts to respond to both domestic critics and the Soviet Union through an expanded defence effort. While Defense Secretary McElroy and other Administration spokesmen were on the defensive, especially against the Democratic senators prominent in seeking the 1960 nomination – Hubert Humphrey, Lyndon Johnson, John Kennedy and Stuart Symington – the general stance of Eisenhower and his deputies probably contributed to relatively calm relations with European governments. Restraint created problems for the President at home but was helpful in the wider international context. This was apparent in the continuing European pressure for an arms-limitation agreement with the Soviets:

At the end of 1957, even in the depths of their anxiety about the implications of the sputniks, the Nato allies had shown themselves willing to accept American intermediate range ballistic missiles (IRBM) only on condition that a renewed effort would be made to reach agreement with the Soviet Union on arms control and a reduction of nuclear tensions.[22]

The Administration nevertheless did expand defence spending noticeably from 1957. The sense of being on the defensive, the diversity of challenges around the globe, the renewed pressures to increase conventional forces, and the powerful political and economic pressures for a strategic nuclear build-up combined to push the Administration in the direction of more defence spending. In many ways, therefore, the work of Eisenhower's last Defense Secretary, Thomas Gates, served as a precursor for what would take place under Robert McNamara.

There was also from 1958 the renewed crisis over Berlin, which seemed to serve as the centrepiece of Khrushchev's strategy of pressure against the West. The Soviets demanded that the status of the surrounded city be changed in such a way that there would be greater integration into the Eastern bloc. Threats, confrontations, tensions and dramatic tests of nerves and resolve at various West German and Berlin checkpoints were the order of the day before the Berlin Wall was constructed in 1961 as the ultimate dramatic answer to the problem of a fleeing population. As analysts frequently note, the problem of the encircled city symbolized the wider dilemma of ideological and military confrontation between East and West.

Finally, the last years of the Eisenhower Administration were troubled by the hostility between Washington and Havana. From early 1959, when Castro's revolution was victorious, there was a very steady deterioration in relations between the two nations. There was no shortage of trouble spots in the world in those years, including parts of Africa and South-east Asia, with attention to them encouraged by the global perspective characteristic of the period. Yet the proximity of Cuba to the United States and, once again, the special flamboyance of the leader, made that issue an especially powerful one in U.S. politics and policy-making.

Naturally, this issue became a major one in the politics of the 1960 campaign for the presidency. In the autumn Kennedy repeatedly returned to this subject in his attacks on Nixon, stressing the theme that the Eisenhower Administration had not been aggressive enough in trying to remove the Castro regime. Nixon in his book *Six Crises* is irritable about this, understandably, arguing that his opponent was able to exploit the situation in a way that the then Vice President, tied to the responsibilities of his executive branch office, could not. Kennedy was very shrewd in stressing the Castro government and the alleged threat to American national security in his own campaign; the presence of a Communist country so close to the United States had by then become a most explosive issue in American politics. Theodore H. White in *The Making of the President 1960*, a volume highly sympathetic to the Kennedy campaign, refers to Castro thus: 'Our slowly deteriorating relations with Fidel Castro of Cuba arrived at a permanent and total hostility as the bearded maniac expropriated American interests in Cuba and welcomed the rocket-rattling support of Mr. Khrushchev from the Kremlin.'[23]

The focus on Cuba, and the growing emphasis on 'doing something' about the Castro regime, served to complicate relations with European allies. Just as the Kennedy Administration would create frictions through the new emphasis on the imperatives of conventional military forces, and renewed emphasis on the need for Europe to do more in Nato, so the new government's preoccupation with eliminating Castro would distance Washington from European capitals. Yet the Eisenhower Administration, if restrained on defence spending, was active in moves to bring down the Cuban government. The Bay of Pigs invasion, carried out at the very start of the Kennedy government, was planned in some detail under Eisenhower.

The effort so directly to eliminate Castro's rule would enrage Europeans on the left and disturb those in the centre, yet the tensions over Cuba within the Alliance were growing almost from the time that Castro's revolution achieved final victory at home. The American trade embargo was resisted by most other nations, including the otherwise generally accommodating British. A fairly innocuous sale of school buses to Cuba was transformed into a central, controversial issue. Castro's regime, which carried out economic nationalization, at least the formalities of land redistribution, and was definitely anti-bourgeois in style, was immediately viewed with sympathy by the ideological left. Even for those who were more moderate in their positions on the ideological spectrum, the picture of Americans alarmed about a nearby Communist government was not one that provoked sympathy. After all, West Europeans had been required to practise that sort of coexistence for well over a decade.

Observers of national political elections in the United States and the priorities that determine outcomes usually see international affairs as less significant than domestic developments. Domestic events, especially the state of the economy, it is said, determine results, not foreign-policy matters. Certainly the national economic recession then taking place adversely affected Nixon. At the same time, the 1960 election, like others before and since, did reflect the impact of international relations as well. Against the conventional wisdom about what is most important in determining election results must be set such developments as Truman's withdrawal from the 1952 campaign and Johnson's similar move in 1968, in both cases because of very unpopular involvement in overseas wars; Eisenhower's very effective use of the peace issue in 1952 and 1956; and, for that matter, Johnson's and Nixon's different use of those concerns in 1964 and 1972. In the 1960 race, Cuba was just one element in a foreign-policy scene that included the Soviet Union's alleged superiority in missiles, the Berlin crisis, sputniks, deterioration of the anti-Communist forces in Laos, and worry about the intentions of China. Kennedy made use of all the elements of concern in his aggressive, ultimately successful, campaign.

Kennedy's election to the White House was not an event that caused joy in the capitals of Western Europe, although, as in the United States, there was some satisfaction within the intellectual community and related professional circles that the Eisenhower Administration was giving way to a different, more activist, apparently more liberal group of leaders. De Gaulle was friendly to Eisenhower, who during the Second World War was virtually the only Allied leader who was friendly to him. Adenauer too was close to the retiring President. Even Macmillan, who would later build a close rapport with Kennedy, must have felt uncertainty as the older American President, so much like the Prime Minister in age and experience, and – again – a man with whom he had been able to work effectively, retired from the scene. All the European leaders could easily remember earlier periods in history, and not just the anguished ones of the 1930s and 1940s, which contrasted markedly and unfavorably with the years of peace, prosperity and usually friendly American leadership under Eisenhower.

If anything, the tendency in recent years to evaluate President Eisenhower more favorably, including his conduct of foreign policy, has further justified the regard with which he was held by other national leaders and not just those in Europe. The President's standing was already secure with the average American. Yet some reservations can be expressed about the Eisenhower years in total. His honesty, concern with peace and economic stability, attention to orderly administration and co-ordination, and protection of the dignity of his office are all important strengths. However the fact remains that during those years the United States was viewed, to some extent accurately and especially during Eisenhower's second term, as insufficiently aggressive in meeting Soviet challenges, not only in Europe but in many other parts of the globe. This did leave Kennedy an opening, which he skilfully developed, both as candidate and President, perhaps in so doing taking policy too far to the other extreme of agitated activism.

3 New Strategies, New Strategists

The Kennedy Administration which assumed power in Washington in 1961 represented a sharp break with the preceding Eisenhower regime not only in public style, but also in operational approaches and to some extent the substance of policy. Arguably, almost every new presidential administration brings to the scene a comparatively immoderate self-image and estimate of the degree to which the future is going to be quite different from the recent past. More than one former aide has commented on the tendency of new presidents to adopt this stance. No doubt some are more conscious of so doing than others. Soon, of course, the great forces of inertia in policy, the precedent of past actions, and the objective restrictions of the international and domestic political environments come into play to circumscribe new courses of action. Hence, even a change in party does not normally bring a true transformation in the overall direction of foreign policy.

Yet the Kennedy Administration was very different from Eisenhower's in several important respects. First, there was the fact that the oldest president to complete a second term in office up until that time was succeeded by the youngest elected president. Theodore Roosevelt had been even younger than Kennedy when he assumed the office following the assassination of President McKinley, and William Henry Harrison and Ronald Reagan were both approximately the age of the departing Eisenhower when they assumed office. Never the less, the contrast in having the undeniably old man followed directly by the uncharacteristically young one was striking, with elements for good – or at least obvious – drama.

Moreover, Kennedy's style very effectively stressed the contrast between his new regime and the promise thereof, and the alleged fatigue of the Eisenhower Administration at its end. The new president had made the theme of 'getting America moving again' a constant refrain of his successful campaign for the White House; his inaugural address mentioned among other things that 'the torch has been passed to a new generation'. It has become virtually a cliché that in his campaign for office Kennedy stressed youth and 'vigour'.[1] And image-building, as both Kennedy and Eisenhower surely appreciated, is a very real part of politics. Both handled that particular genre unusually well; we now understand that point more clearly by the contrast presented by some more recent presidents. In this important dimension, while both were skilful, there was a sharp sense of difference in particulars between the group in power before 1961 and those who arrived that year to replace them.

Second, and related to the earlier point, the new administration in general, and the new president in particular, had an approach to the making of foreign policy which differed markedly from that of the Eisenhower years. This in turn had some bearing on Atlantic-area relations, especially since that part of the world remained of principal concern to Washington. As indicated earlier, Eisenhower clearly saw the value of tight co-ordination to both the planning and the implementation of policy. One of the main criticisms of his years in office was that toward the end planning seemed to become an end in itself, divorced from the practical realities and challenges of policy. Another central feature of the Eisenhower Administration, except at the very end, was the dominance of the Secretary of State in the person of John Foster Dulles.

Kennedy moved with dispatch to change both the foreign-policy structure and the personalities who would be responsible for implementing policy. The large Planning and Operations Co-ordinating Boards, which had been such central features of the Eisenhower years in foreign policy, were abolished in favour of a much smaller National Security Council staff structure. As Special Assistant to the President for National Security Affairs, Kennedy selected McGeorge Bundy, then Dean of the Faculty of Arts and Sciences at Harvard. While Bundy was not the visible figure, or the policy advocate on most questions, to equal some of his successors, he was more assertive in policy and administrative terms than either Gordon Gray or Andrew Goodpaster, his main predecessors during the Eisenhower Administration. Moreover, while arguably not as disorderly as President Lyndon Johnson, or as determined to exercise control as President Nixon – and not as secretive as either – Kennedy did not have Eisenhower's approach of remaining visibly aloof from the process and being seen publicly to intervene only in times of major crisis.

Eisenhower had both strong respect for the institutional proprieties involved in the presidency and a political style which emphasized placing himself above the fray in public perception.

Kennedy by contrast was anxious to be involved, and to be seen to be involved, in a more obvious way. Both Kennedy and Bundy were especially interested in Atlantic and European affairs. Bundy represented the views and style of the Eastern Establisment, which was so drawn toward and influential in Atlantic-area relations. Kennedy's style seemed in some ways more British than American; at least he liked that comparison and readily granted Anglophile tendencies. There was also the continuing reality that those in Washington, and for that matter elsewhere, who were disposed toward foreign-policy analysis saw Europe as the centre of the most serious and dangerous direct confrontation between the two superpowers, a situation symbolized by the continuing Berlin crisis, which spanned the Eisenhower and Kennedy years.[2]

Third – a much more concrete and quantifiable point – this was a time when the fundamental strategic equation between the United States and the Soviet Union was changing. Kennedy was able to exploit the perception that the Soviet Union was growing more assertive in the world and the United States less so; that Moscow was achieving greater success than Washington; and that more effort from Washington in the foreign-policy arena was needed. Part of this reflected the perceived lethargy of the last years of the Eisenhower regime.

There was also the fact that the basic nuclear strategic relationship had changed. The fundamental shift occurred when the Soviets developed the capacity to strike the United States directly with intercontinental ballistic nuclear-armed missiles. This in turn drastically and permanently altered the United States' perceived – and actual – security in the international system in general and *vis-à-vis* the Soviet Union in particular. This new state of affairs placed enormous new strains upon those whose mission was U.S. foreign policy. Into the 1960s, the United States had a substantial lead over the Soviet Union in all objective measurements of nuclear striking capability. However, by the late 1950s the Soviets had acquired the capability to hit the United States with intercontinental bombers, as well as Western Europe through IRBMs. The major breakthrough for the Soviets took place about 1960, when they began to deploy new intercontinental missiles capable of striking the United States.

THE MILITARY EQUATION FOR NATO

As a result, for the first time U.S. guarantees to protect Europe through Nato, using nuclear forces if necessary, became truly doubtful for many Europeans. Would the United States really risk destruction on an unprecedented national scale in general nuclear war in order to keep Europe from Soviet domination? Would the Americans do so if, in particular, the Warsaw Pact chose to rely on conventional forces for a sweep across Europe and was able to carry out such an invasion successfully? American fears about a gradual neutralization of Western Europe through Soviet threats and inducements became much greater after the other side had developed these new, quite menacing strategic capabilities. West Germany became a particular focus for such concern, occupying as it does a pivotal position on the East–West line of demarcation, and susceptible to ploys containing the promise of a reunified Germany. What has been termed in recent years by George Kennan, and then others, as a possible 'Finlandization' of Western Europe became a far more serious worry after the American nuclear monopoly came to an end.

This turning-point was perhaps more crucial, and certainly appeared to be even more worrisome from the point of view of Washington, than contemporary fears about Soviet 'parity' or 'superiority' in nuclear weapons. There is no doubt that more recent years have not witnessed the sense of almost continuous alarm which characterized the Kennedy Administration from the very beginning. In turn, there has perhaps been a tendency to minimize or overlook the enormous perceived pressures under which the decision-makers of the early 1960s were compelled to operate.[3]

This state of affairs helped to bring about a fundamental change in American nuclear strategic doctrine. The 1950s was a time when basic changes took place in the way in which informed professionals thought about the nuclear-weapons environment and debated its implications. The Kennedy Administration brought about practical changes in strategic doctrine and Pentagon organization, both of which reflected the propositions and approaches which had been germinating during the earlier years.

In terms of strategic doctrine, 'massive retaliation' was in formal terms succeeded by 'flexible response'. It had become increasingly difficult to believe that Americans would automatically sacrifice their cities in a general nuclear exchange no matter what the nature of the attack, including a limited conventional war thrust in Europe,

Reasonable people and those initiated into the more arcane concepts of nuclear war and deterrence doctrines both had difficulty with this stance, which offended common sense as well as more sophisticated notions of proportionality and reciprocity. Instead of accepting the inevitability of total devastation, planners sought instead to exercise control of a type which would restrict escalation if possible. Should war break out, violence should be kept to the lowest possible level.

This in turn implied that those who had to make these profound decisions should have a range of different options available to them. This meant maintaining substantial forces of various kinds, nuclear and conventional. The Kennedy Administration therefore was pre-occupied with a military build-up which, though not unplanned or haphazard, was comprehensive, ranging across the board of different kinds of forces. Particular emphasis was given to conventional capabilities, which had been downplayed during the Eisenhower years. The new administration also had a strong interest in unconventional guerrilla and anti-guerrilla efforts, and the U.S. Army's Special Forces, the 'Green Berets'. which had not been encouraged under Eisenhower and were unpopular with the Army establishment, were given considerable attention and support. Concerning strategic forces, there was a powerful movement to make nuclear delivery vehicles as secure as possible, with hardened missile silos for land-based systems and long-range submarines for sea-based systems. The strategic community was victorious; vulnerability was their main preoccupation and the new structure would be designed to permit U.S. systems to 'ride out' a first nuclear strike and retaliate with devastating effect.

In organizational terms, Robert McNamara brought to the Pentagon a commitment to change of the most determined sort, resulting in a profound transformation in the ways in which military policies were made and implemented. He also brought great changes in the ways in which military officers and their civilian counterparts interacted. As one analyst of the defence-budget process has argued, McNamara truly ran the Pentagon, a point which has to be conceded whether or not one agrees with the particular policies he and his colleagues were trying to implement. In reality, some of the management changes effected by McNamara had been anticipated by moves taken by Thomas Gates, Eisenhower's last Secretary of Defense, as noted. Yet, in basic terms, the McNamara revolution really was just that in the impact on Pentagon structure and military doctrine.[4]

The Defense Secretary centralized authority more than ever before in his own office, and much greater emphasis was placed on quantitative statistical indices of performance, actual and anticipated. The Secretary brought with him a series of statistical tools that were generally summed up under the title of 'planning–programming–budgeting'. The system meant among other things that planning and procurement budgets distinguished between different programmes rather than different military services. This was done to try to create a more efficient and also more orderly defence policy and production process. Precise numerical analysis was used in an effort to obtain the best value that could be secured at the price – i.e. the most 'cost-effective' choices were made. These changes were of course undertaken at a time when defence spending generally was being increased very significantly in face of the perceived arms race and wider political competition with the Soviets.

McNamara also brought with him into the Pentagon a team of academically accomplished, quantitatively sophisticated defence analysts who proceeded to employ these control tools. Often disdainful of the career military officers with whom they dealt, possessing more self-confidence than experience, concerned more with clarity than diplomacy, they were made to order to antagonize the Pentagon establishment. The reputation for abrasiveness damaged McNamara's efforts at change at the time and returned to haunt him later when Vietnam came to overshadow U.S. foreign policy generally. His hard-driving approach also served to create almost from the start an alliance of the previously divided military services against the Secretary and his men. There were powerful allies of the military in Congress, which soon developed centres of criticism of the Kennedy Administration's approach to defence policy even in the context of general support for increased spending and the military build-up.

As noted, however, expansion, if controversial in practice, was not undertaken thoughtlessly. There was a sense of priorities and considerable attention to the detailed analysis of strategy; arguably neither has characterized the more recent substantial military-spending growth under President Reagan. The emphasis on conventional forces led to a natural focus on the Army, in contrast to Eisenhower's favouring of the Air Force, the instrument of massive retaliation. General Maxwell Taylor, though no friend of the Special Forces and unconventional warfare, also was at odds with the Army establishment. He had left the service after strong publicized criticism of the Eisenhower priorities. Kennedy brought him back in a key role as military adviser to the President and later Chairman of the Joint Chiefs of Staff.[5]

In terms of strategy, McNamara was especially assertive in articulating the new doctrine as policy. Indeed, initially he went so far as to state that nuclear war itself could be 'managed' effectively to limit damage and perhaps win something resembling a classic military victory. In a major address in Ann Arbor, Michigan, in 1962, the Secretary declared that the United States could in fact target weapon centres rather than cities. This approach to the conduct of a nuclear war would be more rational, more in line with the goal of focusing destruction on military targets rather than civilian population centres, and hence would be more humane. Later, he backed away from this position, in part because targeting strategic weapons may be taken to imply a plan to strike first rather than retaliate, in part perhaps because this extreme conception of control over the development of an actual nuclear war struck him as too theoretical. Certainly others felt this. Yet the larger commitment to rationality of a complex, rather abstract variety in strategic planning remained in place. Conflict, whether conventional or nuclear, was to be as controlled as possible at the start and also throughout. If war could not be prevented, the fighting would be contained at the conventional level. If that nuclear – conventional distinction, which virtually everyone agreed was crucial, should be breached, then exchanges were to be controlled as much as possible, kept 'rational' for as long as possible.[6]

This general approach to strategy had several important consequences for U.S.–European relations. First, the Secretary of Defense became much more visible and broadly influential in U.S. foreign policy. This of course held true whether or not he was advocating a particular course of policy, yet the emphasis on strategic issues and planning, combined with the expansion of American defence spending and force levels under Kennedy, had clear implications for the role and status of the Secretary, who became considerably more important. This was especially possible given the very close working rapport between Kennedy and McNamara, and the consequent leeway granted the latter in both the definition and implementation of defence policy. Like the Secretaries of War and the Navy in earlier times, the defense secretary holds a very senior Cabinet post. He controls the largest single share of the federal budget (and in those years defence spending was a much larger proportion of the total budget and the gross national product than has been the case in more recent years). McNamara himself was quite willing to speak beyond narrow military concerns, reflecting no doubt the restlessness and reach of his intellect, a strong interest in the relations among different components of foreign policy, and also the intense ambition that had brought him to the presidency of the Ford Motor Company at the young age of forty-four.

Kennedy himself praised McNamara strongly from the beginning, in ways that seemed equalled only by Bundy on the White House staff. Certainly McNamara played a broad policy role. The Nassau Conference, held at the end 1962 to try to resolve the controversy with the British over Skybolt, included McNamara in a central capacity; he met with his counterpart Peter Thorneycroft in a preliminary session to try to iron out, or at least define, the differences. It is safe to assume, on this matter and also a range of others, that McNamara had advice for the President on both the political and the military dimensions of the complex equation.[7]

Second, flexible response obviously had important implications for Atlantic-area relations and quickly led to new complications for the partners. European fears were in some ways heightened and made worse. Earlier, Europeans had worried that any conflict might quickly become a nuclear exchange; now they were alarmed that American doctrine meant that Europe could be devastated by conventional warfare while across the ocean the United States remained virtually unscathed. There was further alarm among many Europeans that in a conflict with the Soviets they would provide the conventional military infantry, the Americans the nuclear cavalry held in reserve.

The fact that the Americans' nuclear capacity was so enormous, and the Europeans' so small, made this concern understandable and underscored the basic strategic dependence on the geographically removed, albeit politically involved, superpower ally. To populations which had gone through the agonies of the Second World War, conventional war did not seem so inherently limited. To Europeans preoccupied with economic and political dependence on the Americans, the new doctrine seemed to be one more indication that the superpower could change philosophies at will, unhampered by the reactions of European allies.

This point was underscored by the fact that the vigorous new administration in Washington almost immediately began to press the Europeans to do more in their national military efforts, especially in the conventional field. In fact, the thrust of nuclear arguments emanating from Washington was just the reverse: proliferation was the major threat and the American nuclear monopoly therefore was judged essential. There was an understandable European reluctance to undertake new conventional commitments. Aside from worries about possible replays of Second World War battles in the same theatre of operations, conventional forces undeniably were expensive and many nations were already maintaining rather large conventional forces, not least because of lingering colonial commitments and headaches.

THE ATLANTIC COMMUNITY

The tapestry of relations was further complicated by a new emphasis on 'Atlantic community' among the nations of North America and Western Europe. Beginning in the early 1960s, there was much greater American stress on the possibilities for and the desirability of political integration, not only in Europe but in the wider area of the North Atlantic. This reflected propensities within the Kennedy Administration and also movements growing within informed foreign-policy circles in the United States. In some ways, the new method and mood was continuous with what had gone before. Just as the Kennedy activism in opposing the Soviet Union flowed from the anti-Communism of the Eisenhower years, so too the new concern with structural unification was based upon a more longstanding American commitment to European integration. Eisenhower and Dulles had been supportive of Jean Monnet's vision of a politically united Europe, the *status quo* American administration aligning itself with one of the most ambitious and important political reform movements in post-war Europe.

As with opposition to the Soviets, however, support for Europe was given a new tone and direction by the Kennedy Administration. Rhetoric on the subject was more flowery, less limited. Also, there was a tendency to link America with Europe in a general vision of a broad Atlantic community of politically integrated nations. The Republicans of the 1950s, with the exception of Nelson Rockefeller on the party's left, had avoided these sorts of vision. Speaking in Philadelphia on 4 July 1962, Kennedy gave voice to an emerging Atlantic unity which could be compared with the unification of the original thirteen colonies in the United States.[8]

The ambitions of the Kennedy Administration focused attention on European matters and also created a host of new problems within the Alliance by sharpening strategic tensions. This was the direct result of a much more rigorous approach to defence policy in conceptual terms. Europeans had been unhappy with the Eisenhower policy of massive retaliation because of the promise of great devastation if war broke out; they were now unhappy with flexible response because war might become more likely and also more devastating. Emphasis on conventional defence also seemed to disengage American risks from European risks. A reassertion of American leadership in addition reminded the Europeans of their strong dependence on decisions by and attitudes in Washington. Last, stress on political integration, when there was no institutional structure upon which to base that goal, guaranteed political frustration over the long term.

THE MULTILATERAL FORCE AND SKYBOLT

Different pieces of evidence can be employed to help in developing these points. In military–strategic terms, the Multilateral Force (M.L.F.) and Skybolt experiences have been used to highlight the ways in which dependence resulted in severe problems for the Atlantic Alliance. Reviewing the main components of the crises is useful to our purposes now. In the first case, American efforts to create the form of nuclear decision-sharing only underscored the reality that there was a *de facto* American monopoly in that area. In the latter case, the British 'special relationship' with the United States was shown to contain the seeds of especially severe and humiliating reversals for an international power in decline. In broader political terms, the American efforts at bold, direct leadership provided an opportunity primarily for the French, but also for other independent-minded Europeans, to find room for manoeuvre of their own. The Franco-German friendship treaty of 1963 may be employed to highlight this point. Finally, the events surrounding the progress and lack of progress in development of the European Community, and related negotiations between the Europeans and Americans in the 1960s, can be used to make the case for the propostion that opportunities for great institutional integration in Europe and the Atlantic area were considerably overblown during this period. But with this issue we are moving beyond the events directly involving the 'new strategists' of the Kennedy years.

The M.L.F. originally developed as a State Department initiative to mitigate and respond to building pressures in Europe for a greater European voice in management of the American nuclear deterrent. The spectre of an emerging French nuclear force provided a considerable incentive to U.S. leaders to try to prevent other European nations from following the same path. Concern about nuclear proliferation among industrial – as opposed to developing – nations was a constant theme during this period among those who made as well as those who studied foreign policy. The M.L.F. emerged from deliberations on the best way to bring the Europeans into the command.

Essentially, the M.L.F. plan was for a special fleet of Nato ships to be established, armed with nuclear weapons and served by crews from different Alliance nations. Being at sea would provide some physical security, but the main point was that no nation could exercise direct control over the force. The M.L.F. was originally conceived as a small fleet of submarines, but, with men of so many different nationalities involved, the psychological problems of living and working together in such a confined environment would have been too great, and it was decided to operate with surface ships instead. The fact that vulnerability would be increased through the political requirements of the plan should perhaps have given pause but did not.

The principal author of the M.L.F. scheme was Robert Bowie, who put his ideas in the form of an influential memorandum on the subject in 1960. Bowie had been a close aide to Secretary of State Dulles during the first part of the Eisenhower Administration; hence his initiative carried considerable weight. This was only right, given his intimate involvement in Alliance policy details over a period of years; yet in retrospect the M.L.F. project created unprecedented mischief for concord among the nations involved without any counterbalancing benefits, either political or strategic.

One important spur for the M.L.F. approach was growing worries about the cohesion of the Alliance in the face of increased U.S. vulnerability to nuclear attack and the image of a much more threatening Soviet Union. The successful launching of Sputnik 1 in 1957 not only set off a frenzy of concern in U.S. policy circles about the adequacy of scientific research and development; there was also in practical terms an agreement not long thereafter for Jupiter missiles to go to Britain, Italy and Turkey under an arrangement whereby the United States would retain control of the warheads and both sides could veto use of the weapons. The end of the Eisenhower Administration witnessed various suggestions, including some from Defense Secretary Thomas Gates and Nato Commander Lauris Norstad, for the establishment of different forms of nuclear forces formally under Alliance control.

Unfortunately for both the Americans' prestige and broader Alliance concord, the M.L.F. initiative was from the beginning dogged by lack of clarity about goals and purposes. Many different pressures within the Kennedy Administration propelled the M.L.F. forward, and to a striking degree they were not consistent. The force was backed by those who were interested principally in promoting cohesion in Alliance relations, but some were more concerned for a strong integrated Europe, others much more with keeping Europe within the domain of the United States.

Henry Kissinger was an especially telling, and visible, critic of the inconsistencies and tensions inherent in the proposal, which slowly but steadily rose to the surface of the discussion. After a term as a consultant to the Kennedy Administration, an experience that was by various accounts unhappy and frustrating, Kissinger found himself on the outside looking in at policy, increasingly concerned about the course being pursued with regard to European affairs. Certainly his experience within the corridors of power added insight to his views; perhaps the interpersonal problems involved coloured his conclusions. Never the less, they wear well with time:

> The pressures of a relatively small group of officials in the State Department gave our Allies a misleading impression of American unanimity and commitment. The Pentagon had accepted the M.L.F. only on the assumption that ultimate American control would remain unimpaired. The group in the State Department that originated the M.L.F. proposal and pressed it on our Allies was much more sympathetic to the ultimate emergence of a separate European nuclear force. Indeed, it occasionally urged the M.L.F. as a means to this end. Although the cohesiveness of our society depends on understanding conflicting views, it is dangerous to engage in major international innovations unless we are clear about our ultimate direction.[9]

A similar lack of clarity surrounded notions of how the M.L.F. would affect the roles and positions of various nations within the Alliance. France was to be restrained through the mechanism of the M.L.F. The French nuclear force, a great preoccupation of policy-planners in Washington, would effectively be absorbed through the larger collective nuclear military effort. Yet the M.L.F. was also sup-posed to enhance the European dimension of Nato. There was at least a superficial paradox in trying to enlarge the role of Europe while diminishing the roles of the individual European nation states. The West German hand would be strengthened, explicitly and decisively, through access to nuclear weapons in the context of this force. Immediately, other nations in Europe became very nervous. The

British, for example, were drawn to the force by their desire to limit the new West German influence. Franco-German co-operation was one reason why the Americans promoted the M.L.F. yet France and West Germany would remain colleagues on nuclear matters if the new force came into being and also if it did not, in terms of peaceful uses of nuclear power.

To quote Kissinger again,

> Perhaps these aims were not irreconcilable. But because an explicit consideration of them was avoided in favour of the technical problems of mixed-manning, the debate in the winter of 1964 was mortgaged by many previous evasions and ambiguities, some of them deliberate.[10]

As has happened in other policy areas, the Americans turned to emphasis on technical details in lieu of, as an easy substitute for, more extensive strategic political calculations. In this area as in others, the lack of non-technical analysis in depth ultimately defeated the exercise.

The image of independence for the force was of course pure illusion from the start. At the very beginning, the Americans made clear that they would hold back the vast bulk of their own strategic deterrent from integration into the force. Also, every nation involved in the effort had an effective veto over use of the M.L.F. missiles. In reality, the American strategic force remained both preponderant and independent. The Europeans would under the U.S. plan effectively be restricted to the small British and French nuclear forces and the symbolic M.L.F. controlled completely by no one and limited in effect entirely by American decision.[11]

These considerations and others led President Johnson to remove American pressure on European allies to implement the M.L.F. option. His administration ended the initiative for the force as a solution to the range of Alliance tensions and woes. The M.L.F. has not since re-emerged as an idea for serious consideration within Nato. Part of this no doubt reflects an ultimately clear appreciation of the inherent contradiction of the approach. There is also the point, however, that worries about proliferation among the Atlantic nations have appeared to wane over time. The danger is felt much less acutely than in the mid-1960s, when Richard Neustadt could paint scenarios of several Cuban missile crises taking place simultaneously as a result of the increased number of nuclear actors on the stage.[12] Indeed, the fact that proliferation has continued, but very slowly, may well have diminished rather than aggravated fears of the dangers inherent in the trend. Instead, collective attention within Nato has since been focused elsewhere, on other problems.

The second major Alliance crisis, the Anglo-American controversy over the Skybolt missile, was more attenuated and involved only two Nato partners, but this does not make it less significant for an understanding of wider relations and problems among the Atlantic nations. The implications of this particular drama stretch beyond simply Britain and the United States, and the reverberations of the crisis had more general results as well.

Skybolt by the early 1960s had become the centrepiece of British strategic nuclear planning even as the system had become more and more peripheral to the Americans. Eisenhower, usually if not always inclined to be sympathetic to the British view, had made an informal commitment to his friend Prime Minister Harold Macmillan that the United States would supply the weapon which had become so essential. In British planning, Skybolt, based upon this tenuous promise, became crucial for extending the life of the 'V' series of bombers. The cancellation of the British Blue Streak missile programme made Skybolt vital.

The Kennedy Administration, however, had no such commitment in mind. Indeed, on the evidence, the senior officials in Washington responsible gave very little thought to the implications for London when they decided to scrap the programme in 1962. The decision was taken mainly on grounds of cost-effectiveness rather than diplomacy. The final decision, made in November, perhaps reflected the extraordinary pressures attendant on the Cuban Missile Crisis of the previous month. In fairness to those who made the final choices on the matter, Eisenhower's officials had apparently left only a rather sketchy description in the formal record of what had been agreed upon. This was unusual where that particular president was concerned, and for anyone reflecting on the issues could only have reinforced the impression that this was not a major matter for either side and in any case had not yet been decided one way or the other. Skybolt had by this time failed a number of important tests and was regarded as less accurate, less reliable and less effective than other weapons at the disposal of the Americans.

The decision would have been disastrous at any time for Harold Macmillan, but the timing turned out to be especially unfortunate in

the context of the broader British domestic political scene of 1962.
John Baylis, in his comprehensive treatment of Anglo-American
relations since the Second World War, notes that '1962 had been a bad
year for the British Prime Minister'. He goes on to describe the
pressures and problems:

> The introduction of a pay-pause, the unpopular application to join
> the European Economic Community, electoral defeats, the sacking
> of a third of the Cabinet together with criticism over the British role
> in the Cuban crisis, had significantly tarnished the 'super Mac'
> image.[13]

An acrimonious meeting between McNamara and British Defence
Minister Peter Thorneycroft was followed by the winter summit at
Nassau just before Christmas. The political temperature was further
lowered by a speech by former Secretary of State Dean Acheson at
West Point, where he made his immediately famous statement that the
British had lost an empire yet not found a suitable new role in the
world. Much arcane and debatable language was put into the final
communiqué from Nassau relating to distinctions and justifications for
national and 'multinational' use of nuclear weapons. In point of fact,
however, the agreement underscored that Britain could no longer,
seriously and realistically, claim status as a great international military
power. Economic decline had finally been brought home with a
vengeance by its impact on Britain's independent standing in the
world. No great power could have fundamental security so unsettled
by the decisions of another. In any particular crisis, the British could
decide on their own to use their Polaris force to strike the Soviet union
or elsewhere. In political terms, however, the British were now
obviously dependent on American support and generosity. Military
reality was congruent with the basic political decision taken in London
years before to co-ordinate closely with Washington. Yet the British
wanted to maintain too the fiction that London still represented a
power centre separate from Washington and Moscow in the nuclear
imagery and gamesmanship of the 1950s and 1960s. Skybolt and
Nassau put an end to that illusion. As one student of the period
observed, 'The two events that underlined the decline of Britain's
influence in Washington most vividly were the Suez crisis and the
cancellation of the Skybolt missile.'[14]
De Gaulle clearly understood this reality, which anyway reinforced

his image of the international system and the price of American dominance, and he reacted coldly to Anglo-American overtures after the conclusion of the Nassau agreement. The French were offered the same Polaris terms as the British – the missiles if they could supply the warheads and build the submarines to carry them. An analyst had summed up de Gaulle's reaction this way: 'De Gaulle said, in effect, that the offer had no interest for France as long as it did not include what the U.S. already had assisted Britain to obtain – the know-how for building nuclear submarines and warheads for the missile.' Both Kennedy and his ambassador in Paris had been noncommittal on such technical assistance to the French.[15]

The same observer has argued that the British and Americans perhaps could have achieved a more positive result with a different approach. Initially, it appears, de Gaulle was interested in possible co-operation along the lines suggested. After all, the notion of a three-power directorate of Nato, involving close co-operation between Washington, London and Paris, had been floated by the General himself soon after returning to power. A nuclear directorate based on the Nassau agreement would be one possible way to achieve this goal. De Gaulle expressed some interest to U.S. Ambassador Charles Bohlen in talks on 4 January 1963. Kennedy and Macmillan decided in *de facto* terms on a public approach of publishing the Nassau accord and sending a copy to de Gaulle with a brief covering letter.

> If, indeed, the two statesmen had flown from Nassau to Paris to discuss the plan before it was hardened by public release, it is conceivable that they could have succeeded, at the very least, in opening a prolonged negotiation that might have covered Britain's entry into the Common Market. Succeed or fail, the effort would have been worthwhile, once the decisions had been taken to offer the Polaris both to Britain and France.[16]

This course was not taken, and therefore speculation about what might have been remains moot. None the less, the rigidity that came to characterise relations between Paris and Washington during this period is striking, especially since Kennedy (if not de Gaulle) proved himself a very flexible politician in dealing with events, international and domestic. Both Kennedy and de Gaulle were capable of seeing the national interest in mosaic terms. It is curious that they could not reach a more effective accommodation. This provides testimony for the proposition that de Gaulle's intense nationalism and Kennedy's emphasis on an emerging Atlantic community of nations were simply too starkly contrasting to be complementary.

LESSONS OF CRISIS

Two general observations come to mind in reflecting on these policy developments of the turbulent early 1960s. First, the new administration in Washington was not facing a situation fundamentally different from that which had confronted Eisenhower officials. Yet the tensions between the American and European allies grew. To some extent, this can be explained in terms of the new emphasis in a comparatively intellectual administration on conceptual rigour. This sharpened differences of viewpoint, highlighted disagreements whether or not they were likely to be resolved through diplomatic means. Relatedly, the emphasis on quantitative methods for evaluation and ultimate decision downgraded more subtle political calculations. This criticism, so often made of McNamara's tenure at the Pentagon, is symbolized by Skybolt but also can be seen in the M.L.F. – an approach which ignored or brushed aside cultural differences, the varying ways in which the world is seen from different national capitals, and the manner in which a sort of logical clarity in the eyes of one beholder can be suspect as a political form of sleight of hand in the eyes of others.

Second, the concrete military–strategic reality, as opposed to other realities, did not change greatly during this period, except that the Americans launched a major long-term build-up in strategic nuclear forces. The United States retained a clear lead over the Soviet Union in numbers of nuclear missiles and warheads throughout the period of debate and fear over the alleged 'missile gap'. The siege mentality which afflicted Washington, helped to define the political debate in the United States and drove security policy, ensured that the country would remain ahead of the Soviets. As Desmond Ball has argued in his comprehensive analysis of strategic policy under Kennedy,

This illusion of a missile gap was created, nurtured, and maintained by the numerous Americans who feared that the Soviet superiority would lead to a devasting attack on U.S. retaliatory forces. It was in response to the same forces and factors which were responsible for the belief in the missile gap that the Eisenhower Administration increased the U.S. strategic missile program during 1957–60.[17]

While the Eisenhower Administration began the build-up, under Kennedy the pace accelerated and the specifics were defined. To quote Ball further,

> The U.S. strategic missile force reached its present level of 1,000 Minuteman ICBMs [intercontinental ballistic missiles], 54 Titan II ICBMs, and 41 FBN submarines carrying 656 Polaris missiles during the last half of 1967; the development of each of these missile systems was begun under the Eisenhower Administration, but the decisions as to force levels, strategic mix, type of deployment, associated strategy, and so on, were made by the Kennedy Administration. Only a dozen of the primitive first-generation Atlas D ICBMs and two Polaris FBN submarines had been deployed when the Kennedy Administration took office.[18]

In this sense, the Kennedy Administration, with the clarity hindsight always provides, can be faulted for going so far in the strategic build-up. In retrospect, the restraint of the Eisenhower Administration seems more attractive. Only after the strategic build-up under Kennedy was under way did the Soviets visibly begin their own relentless expansion of forces. Knowing what is now available about the character of Soviet forces at the end of the 1950s, the United States should have limited its own expansion.

Yet again the political context, in this case the domestic atmosphere in which policy is made, cannot be slighted. The belief was increasingly widespread, among the general public as well as the experts, and not just in the United States, that the Soviets were gaining a significant military advantage. Not to be underestimated either is the strong Congressional pressure on both Kennedy and McNamara for an even greater build-up; the Defense Secretary at one point remarked that 1000 Minuteman missiles was the minimum number that would be agreed to by Congress. To have tried for less would probably have meant having to accept more. The Soviets already were perceived as being more assertive and successful on the international political stage, especially in the competition for the sympathies of the emerging states of the third world but also in the direct confrontation between the superpowers themselves and between their European security alliances. This was the dominant sentiment of the time, and the Kennedy Administration shared and was responsive to those views, just as the President as candidate had successfully exploited these feelings, not just regarding the 'missile gap', during the 1960 compaign.[19]

During this period, too, strategic rather than economic issues dominated the landscape of relations among Nato members. The balance of payments had only just begun to cause concern. Direct trade balances were of no particular worry to Washington. So strong was American dominance of the international economy, and so secure were such multilateral institutions as the I.M.F., that the United States with confidence bordering on complacency could encourage the formation of a European Common Market that would be more clearly protectionist in trade practices and policies. The goal of political unification, and integration of West Germany into the wider European political tapestry, was much more important to an economic superpower that did not yet have to worry much about the effects of foreign competition. In so far as the Administration was interested and involved in international economics, the emphasis was on the positive side of reduction of tariff barriers and promotion of freer trade through what ultimately came to be titled the 'Kennedy Round' of trade negotiations.

BILATERAL DEVELOPMENTS

At the same time, the issues at hand were not simply strategic in nature, and the main crisis did not revolve entirely around such collective strategic notions as the M.L.F. The Kennedy years also witnessed a series of bilateral conflicts and other political developments involving the United States and each of its major European allies. The manner in which the Administration dealt with these problems defines and highlights important qualities of Atlantic-area relations during the early 1960s.

First, in the case of Great Britain, the major crisis created by the cancellation of the Skybolt missile programme had implications for the bilateral realtionship between the two allies as well as for the wider Nato system. What remains to be stressed is the manner in which good personal rapport between Kennedy and Macmillan contributed directly to larger concord, kept such problems as the Skybolt crisis from being more damaging and extended the life of British influence with Washington (if not of the bomber-based British nuclear deterrent). Kennedy's first meeting with the British Prime Minister after achieving the White House did not go well. The schedule was apparently rushed and the tone of discussion tense. However, later the two were able to establish increasingly close personal rapport. Despite the difference in age, political styles and interests were not all that different. Kennedy consulted the British Prime Minister thereafter with some regularity, having a number of telephone conversations with him during the Cuban Missile Crisis.[20]

Unfortunately, good personal relations did not translate readily into more generally effective policy co-operation. Macmillan finally persuaded the Conservative Party to accept the European Economic Community as a major political, not just economic, reality for Britain. The party did at long last accept the course of formal application for membership of the organization. This did not, however, mean success. The rhetoric from various quarters, not just within the Kennedy Administration, about an emerging 'United States of Europe' could not change the fundamental political reality of Gaullist opposition to British entry. How much the Nassau imbroglio contributed to the ultimate French rejection of the British application can only be surmised; certainly the timing of Nassau could not have been worse from this perspective. De Gaulle for his own purposes stressed that factor, but his antipathy to the 'Anglo-Saxons' was by then long-established and very well known. All that can be determined with certainty is that by 1963 the British had been reminded most dramatically that they were going to have to struggle hard to enter an organization that they could have joined easily at the time of formation.[21]

Underscored as well was the lesson that close amity between Washington and London, and between the heads of the two governments as individuals, was not enough to guarantee easy relations with the rest of Europe. In earlier years, the British had effectively served as a catalyst to bring the Americans into direct, profound political and economic engagement with a devastated Europe. Now, Europe's rediscovery of its own independent identity meant that the 'special relationship' between the British and the Americans was as much a liability as an asset for the former in trying to deal with the other West European states.

Another point which emerges in reflecting on the course of Anglo-American relations during this period is that the Nassau crisis was uniquely troubling not just because of the strength of the special relationship, but also because Britain's decline meant there were comparatively few other issues on which it was likely to disagree with the United States. Had Britain remained a great imperial power, there is little doubt that there would have been a range of conflicts between the two nations, just as there had been at earlier periods in this complex relationship. The British decline had progressed, however, to the point where there was very little basis for serious conflict beyond that related to helping the nation maintain a greater nuclear force than would otherwise have been possible.

Moreover, the British generally handled their shrinking international involvements effectively, skilfully moving power from imperial to national bases in areas where they formally had been dominant. In contrast to the French, and especially the Dutch and Portuguese, the British generally recognized when the time had come to let go. This freed dwindling resources, intellectual as well as economic, for involvement elsewhere, notably in Europe, and again avoided problems with Washington. Finally, the British had for so long placed emphasis on good relations with the United States, and had been so attentive to their side of the special relationship, that by the early 1960s this approach had become virtually second nature to them. If there were to be major disruptions, these would come from the American side.

Diverse and heavy international obligations also come to the forefront when considering the ways in which the British might have dramatically altered their role. Critics have frequently focused on the reluctance of the British to change their style and expectations in the international system following the Second World War. To be sure, Suez was a genuine fiasco, involving total miscalculation about the American response; Skybolt is a striking example of misperception of American policy intentions; and the British can be accused generally of lack of foresight in the conduct of their policies, especially regarding the European Community. Yet, arguably, conceptually clear foresight has never been a hallmark of British foreign policy. Rather, as more perceptive analysts have observed, the British specialize instead in moving flexibly with events, displaying a supremely non-ideological approach to policy and developments. This was the quality which permitted them to play so effective a role as classic balancer in the international power system of the sixteenth to eighteenth centuries, and to provide such a moderating influence not only against the revolutionary tides unleashed by Napoleon but also against the conservative counter-revolution which Austria led following his defeat.[22]

Had the British moved more dramatically and explicitly to recognize national limitations and protect primary national interests – perhaps through adopting the role of a Sweden or Switzerland – there would probably have been greater disruptions to the lives of smaller nations elsewhere. The obverse of the problem of the British being slow to move into Europe, and to recognize primary economic interests there, was that they were a continuing stabilizing force in former colonial areas. Part of the reason why policy was so slow to change was that the nation had so many different obligations well beyond Europe. Thanks to continuation of reasonably friendly relations with many former colonial areas, there were lingering security commitments following the end of colonial status.

And the British have performed impressively in a variety of limited armed conflicts resulting from such ties. The British victory in the Falklands War is a particularly dramatic but not unique example of the effective application of military force in limited conflicts. Earlier, in the1960s, there were successful military engagements in both Aden and Malaysia, and the earlier conflict in Malaya in the 1940s and early 1950s. No longer a great imperial power, the nation has demonstrated a continuing capacity for military prowess in former, and a few continuing, colonial areas. The British record, undramatic when compared with the extraordinary past (and a past somewhat over-dramatized as well), is therefore fairly easy to underestimate. Yet the manner in which adjustment has been made from great power to middle power, without significant foreign or domestic disruptions, has been handled with deceptive smoothness.

The Federal Republic of Germany presented a stark contrast to Britain in political and military history, contemporary political position and strategic problems, and so it is not surprising that the relationship Washington had with Bonn in the early 1960s was in some contrast to the relationship with London. The Kennedy Administration confronted in Germany some particularly serious problems, reflecting Konrad Adenauer's unique role in defining the place of his country in the Atlantic area, in Europe and, perhaps most important of all, in the eyes of his fellow citizens. Eisenhower, ever able to deal effectively on the interpersonal level, had formed a good working relationship with de Gaulle and was able to do the same with the West German Chancellor. Eisenhower's interpersonal skills, which had been so vital to the Allied war effort, continued to pay dividends in foreign policy. Dulles was an obvious and unapologetic Germanophile. After literally years of comfortable rapport with the top leaders in Washington, and keenly aware of his own significance in establishing the Federal Republic as a cohesive national entity as well as a responsible Nato ally, Adenauer quickly chafed at the policy approaches of the new regime in Washington.

Kennedy, while able to develop good rapport with Macmillan, did not have similar success with Adenauer. The personal contact between the two apparently served only to reinforce rather than mitigate Adenauer's negative feelings about the new American leadership. Perhaps no U.S. President could have overcome the West German Chancellor's increasing sensitivities and irritability as his long, distinguished career drew toward a close. None the less, the Kennedy Administration must have appeared particularly brash and difficult from his point of view. The constant emphasis on new approaches and new departures could be interpreted as a form of denigration of a postwar past in which Adenauer had played such a central role. Certainly in stylistic terms there was little in common between the President and the Chancellor, and the contrast and frictions must have been especially grating to a German leader who had become accustomed to such good rapport with the earlier regime.

Policies and crises served further to complicate German–American relations during these years. Berlin's position seemed to become even more precarious, in turn placing pressures on the two Western governments principally involved. Very early in Kennedy's term, he was confronted with the Berlin Wall, a dramatic Soviet solution to the problem of migration of the population of East Germany toward the West and one for which there was no effective Western riposte. The Bay of Pigs fiasco, again very early in Kennedy's tenure, must have created further insecurity about the quality and reliability of the American leadership. The Vienna summit meeting between Kennedy and Khrushchev provided further shocks to the sense of Alliance stability. Kennedy tried to deal effectively with the Soviet leader, but he did not respond in kind to the bullying tactics he confronted, and the impression became widespread that the meeting had worsened relations between the two sides rather than improving matters. Kennedy himself noted that apparently the Western allies were in for 'a long, cold winter' and he was prompted to go on U.S. television to describe to the nation the gravity of the tensions between the two blocs. Reportedly, Khrushchev was sufficiently unimpressed by the American leader to feel that he could go ahead with his plans to move strategic missiles into Cuba the following year.[23]

The West Germans could not have been happy with the American emphasis on 'flexible response' either. The considerations which led Europeans in general to be un-enthusiastic about the approach applied with particular significance to West Germany. To Europeans, with memories of the devastation of the Second World War still fresh, conventional war was a reality that was very destructive, as Germans in particular had cause to know. Moreover, West Germany was aleady contributing a very large percentage of Nato's ground forces, and the request to do even more in the conventional field seemed to imply a lack of appreciation for what had already been devoted to the cause. Finally, the Central Front in Europe, the area of most likely immediate fighting between Nato and the Warsaw Pact, ran right through Germany. Thus, the new emphasis on conventional deterrence and 'flexible response' seemed to undercut rather than reinforce West German security. Certainly the point was made strongly that Germany would provide the battleground in a general war between the two blocs. Also, stress on conventional forces was taken to imply that perhaps the war costs in human terms would be borne primarily by the Germans while the Americans were relatively secure.

These pressures and others led to a gap between Bonn and Washington which de Gaulle moved rather deftly to fill. Memories of the historic antagonism between France and Germany, which had played key roles in the two world wars, were also still fresh in the early 1960s. Moreover, while de Gaulle was the ultimate nationalist (and perhaps the ultimate dramatist on the international stage besides), Adenauer was for understandable reasons much more positive about the benefits to Europeans of the security tie to the Americans. He was much more sympathetic, at least in principle, to notions of general co-operation within the Atlantic community of nations.

Yet by 1963 antagonism to Washington was sufficiently great for the West German Chancellor to be willing to undertake a treaty of peace and friendship with France. The treaty was a signal victory for de Gaulle, combining the immediate satisfaction of tying Bonn more closely to Paris, and thus less closely to Washington, with the longer-term goal of accommodation between the two old West European adversaries. Kennedy for his part – and to his credit – was philosophical and not entirely negative about these developments. He reminded his policy-makers that a basic goal of U.S. foreign policy toward Europe was to tie West Germany more closely into the wider Western community and alliance structures. 'Now de Gaulle is doing that his own way', he observed.[24] Indeed, a bilateral alliance between France and Germany was useful to Washington in this sense, and far more meaningful in practical political terms than the grand vision of an emerging Atlantic community of nations which was so prominent during the Kennedy years in Washington.

DE GAULLE

Relations between Paris and Washington were particularly strained, if especially colourful, during the early 1960s. The political fencing between Kennedy and de Gaulle was good theatre, and not necessarily entirely negative for Alliance concord. At the most abstract, inclusive level, the disagreement between France and the United States amounted to nothing less than very different conceptions about how the history of national development was moving in the West. According to a dominant strain of opinion in policy circles in Washington and elsewhere, the formation of the European Economic Community had been part of a much more profound movement toward political integration through the formation of supranational institutions. The eventual political unification of Europe would be followed by ever-closer co-operation, and eventual merging, between Western Europe and North America. The vision was most ambitious, and perhaps appropriate to the reform-minded and change-minded early 1960s. As we have seen, the Kennedy Administration became strongly indentified with this point of view.

By contrast, de Gaulle stood solidly with traditional European diplomacy, which emphasized the importance and the permanence of the individual nation state. Seen as an irritant and inflexible by other European and by American leaders, the French President was in fact a defender of the *status quo* and conservative international values. In a revolutionary age, in which not all visionaries were to be found in the third world or among Communist leaders, he was in reality arguing for continuity rather than radical transformation.

Ultimately de Gaulle was correct in his understanding of the forces of history as they played on Alliance relations in the Atlantic area. The notion of an emerging supranational Atlantic community, and for that matter the concept – more precise and therefore striking – of an evolving United States of Europe, were both proved erroneous by events. The idea of an Atlantic community seemed truly to come to an end with the passing of the Kennedy Administraion, when a much less conceptually inclined, much more domestically oriented, American President found himself moving in other directions, responding to his own policy ambitions at home as well as being sucked inexorably into an increasingly costly war in South-east Asia. De Gaulle was also right about the character of the European Community, which became increasingly mired in the resistance of national members to sacrifice of sovereignty over decisions regarding fundamental military and political interests. As we shall see, the reasons why the goal of European political integration was frustrated reach well beyond French intractability or the specific vetoes of British applications for membership. So the main contribution of the French President, despite his somewhat quixotic image, was to remind Europeans and Americans of basic, if unpleasant, political realities.

De Gaulle also performed more specific services for his nation and the wider Atlantic system of states, linked to the basic thrust of French policy under his leadership. First, he was able to carry out an institutional revolution within the French political system which continues to the present time. The revolving-door national governments of the French Fourth Republic were replaced with not just a leader who was generally respected and charismatic, but also a set of institutions which were designed to bolster and legitimize national political power. The constitution of the Fifth Republic did not remove the president from politics; if anything, he was made a more important, because more clearly defined, participant. The new institutions gave him an existence apart from the fractious legislature which had been the bane of earlier French premiers and cabinets. The seven-year presidential term gave the national executive a separate power base and sufficient time for a major impact on policies and events. The president was provided the freedom to communicate directly with the people beyond the legislature, as de Gaulle (like Napoleon) did so well. The president was also granted a very substantial panoply of executive powers, which might threaten eventual dictatorship, owing to such mechanisms as control over the national media, but which if respected would avoid the chronic weaknesses of the Fourth Republic.

Second, de Gaulle as a unique cultural figure was able to re-establish a sense of positive national identity. So significant was his accomplishment in restoring French pride and self-confidence, that one can easily overlook the fact that during the late 1940s and 1950s France was generally and rightly regarded as the political 'sick man' of Western Europe, beset with instability of both policies and governments. When France was able to undertake co-operative ventures, as in the Suez strike of 1956, the results seemed to damage further rather than help the national position. France was overshadowed by both Britain, representing continuity with past influence and power, and West Germany, with its new strength and confidence. Given this situation, de Gaulle's exceptional ego, and the inconvenience resulting from

French military independence from the Nato command, were small prices to pay for a much more stable and secure, and hence reliable, partner in the Alliance.

Third, de Gaulle through guile and force was able to cut away the lingering problems around the globe that served to weaken French diplomacy. If his traditionalist perspective meant that he thought in terms of great-power diplomacy in the context of Europe, that was congruent with the pressing contemporary need to lift the burdens of old colonialism. Hence, with striking ruthlessness, he separated himself from the military colleagues who had been so important in his return to power, moving instead to grant Algeria independence. The corrupting, indecisive guerrilla warfare there which had undercut the Fourth Republic was suddenly over. In a similar manner, de Gaulle worked to focus national attention on Europe and the Atlantic area. If he had his own visions – and 'Europe from the Atlantic to the Urals' certainly qualifies in terms of abstract generality – he at least focused national attention on the region of the world where the main national interest lay. Arguably, in such a fractionated political culture, where events had constantly undercut both policies and governments in the past, such an abrupt and dramatic approach to change was necessary. The French probably would have failed had their approach been that of the gradualist, accommodating British.

THE KENNEDY YEARS: AN ASSESSMENT

These were the currents which challenged the Kennedy Administration in the Atlantic area, and in different ways the American leadership served to churn the waters further, antagonizing already strained relations, at least in the case of West Germany and probably in that of France as well. Does this mean that the judgement on this brief presidential administration should be negative in terms of Atlantic-area political and security relations? Not really: the accurate portrait of policy, and its requirements, is far more complex and subtle. To be sure, in retrospect there were some counterproductive aspects to the Kennedy Administration's general approach to allies and adversaries. The impatience, the constant stress on action, and a tone which was at times strident and indeed belligerent look less impressive now than they did at the time. Also, the emphasis on reassertion of American leadership in the Atlantic area and the wider world, a theme which was helpful politically to the President at home, underscored to allies that Washington was interested in control as much as, and perhaps more than, true partnership.

Moreover, at least early in the Kennedy Administration, the President and his colleagues were injured further by the perception that the strident tone was combined with weakness in action. The Bay of Pigs was a genuine disaster and, while reports on the Vienna summit vary, the impression that lingered was that the Soviet Premier was not greatly impressed by his younger counterpart. Even the Cuban Missile Crisis, which has normally been regarded as Kennedy's finest hour in the field of foreign affairs, has come to be viewed by some in a different light. We now know better than we did at the time how threatening the American strategic nuclear build-up of ICBMs and Polaris submarines must have appeared to the Soviets, who were then still struggling to establish their own strategic missile force. Also, there were very strenuous clandestine efforts by Kennedy officials to overthrow Castro and remove the Communist regime in Cuba. In this sense, the Bay of Pigs, far from representing a culmination of sorts, was the beginning of an energetic drive to eliminate Castro. Soviet actions in trying to rush missiles into Cuba are today more understandable, if not defensible.

All of this overlooks the much more positive dimensions of the Kennedy Administration's approach to foreign policy, some of which have particular bearing on Europe. Again, arguably in more recent years this part of the picture has been slighted more than it was in the past. First, and perhaps most important for reflections on Atlantic-area relations, the Kennedy Administration was rightly congruent with the Eisenhower and for that matter the Truman Administration in emphasis on the vital importance of European affairs for U.S. foreign policy generally and in commitment to wider and more effective involvement with Europe's future. Had Kennedy in fact been the total unilateral adventurer that some of his critics contend, there would not have been the stress on various mechanisms for more effective co-operation between North American and Europe. The fact that some of these, notably the M.L.F., did not work well or were shown ultimately to be impractical should not detract from the significance of Washington's association with the goal of co-operation. If the President and his men were at times too sweepingly visionary (in the stress on an emerging 'United States of Europe', among other things) and too assertive for the taste of some senior European leaders (notably de Gaulle and Adenauer), they at least were alive to the possibilities of alliance leading to more inclusive concord among the nations involved.

In more cynical and frustrated times, we perhaps tend to gloss over the value of this quality which the Kennedy Administration brought with particular energy to the conduct of diplomacy.

We also arguably tend to forget that in the late 1950s Europeans, especially among the elite, shared American concern that the Soviets were overtaking the West in both concrete military terms and in more abstract, but important, areas of diplomatic assertiveness and manoeuvre. Khrushchev was viewed as both reckless and powerful, and he and his associates seemed to have the initiative around Berlin, in the wider arena of superpower fencing for advantage and influence, and in the international system generally, especially among the increasingly numerous collection of third-world states.

Kennedy was able effectively to counteract this trend through a combination of political assertiveness and renewed emphasis on military strength. This can be seen as stabilizing in restoring a rough balance between the stances and images of the two superpowers. It is difficult persuasively to argue that the fault for international tensions lay completely in Washington, given the attitude of the Soviet leadership of the day. In more concrete military terms, the Kennedy–McNamara strategic build-up was excessive given Soviet capabilities, but this was not clear at the time. And the Kennedy Administration's contribution went beyond simply increasing military spending. McNamara early in his tenure set his young systems-analysis staff to work on fresh evaluations of the true balance of forces between Nato and the Warsaw Pact countries. The conclusion of this effort was that Nato was not in fact inferior to the other side, that the two blocs were roughly on a par in terms of actual conventional military strength. This was a state of affairs some analysts had guessed at given the amount of money the United States and other Nato members were spending on defence, but the official and more general public perceptions had been quite different.

Second, the pragmatism and flexibility of the Kennedy Administration in handling various international problems has again been slighted in more recent years, but at the time stood in marked contrast to the rigidity and inflexible anti-Communism which characterized the approach to foreign policy of Secretary of State John Foster Dulles under President Eisenhower. And Dulles was usually the spokesman for Eisenhower Administration foreign policy if not – another point we know better than we did then – the final decision-maker in the foreign policy crises of the 1950s. If Kennedy's policy-making and implementation system was not so orderly as Eisenhower's, owing to Kennedy's wish to be clearly 'involved' in the policy process, it was one which was open to new approaches and new ideas. Various analysts have commented on the President's curiosity and open mind concerning policy options and possibilities, a virtue which seems especially striking when compared to the intense secretiveness of Kennedy's two immediate successors in the White House.

In practical terms, this meant that damage could be limited by a president who was willing and able to intervene quickly to overcome misunderstandings. Skybolt demonstrates this point and also the fact that the more orderly, careful Eisenhower approach was hardly infallible. After the Franco-German treaty of friendship of 1963 had been signed, the President was sufficiently flexible to see that this was one way of binding the Germans more closely into the larger Western community, a prime U.S. foreign-policy objective. The Cuban Missile Crisis may be more understandable now in terms of Soviet motives, but that is not to argue that a more passive U.S. response would have led to a more stable balance between the two superpowers. A flexible style, a pragmatic approach, could limit damage and respond to events quickly, even if the possibility of error was greater.

Third, the organizational arrangements of the Kennedy Administration in foreign policy were not in fact so disorderly. The President had fewer formal meetings of the National Security Council, the Cabinet and other bodies, the N.S.C. staff was reduced in size, and various foreign-policy committees were abolished or ignored. Yet there was no effort strictly to centralize foreign policy in the White House. Certainly McGeorge Bundy did not have the dominant role that Kissinger later assumed, by various accounts did not seek such a role, and, if more visible than predecessors under Eisenhower, was considerably more self-effacing than some more recent occupants of the job of security assistant. Perhaps the strongest criticism that can be made of the President in these bureaucratic terms is that he did not sufficiently restrain an aggressive secretary of defense to strictly defence and military-policy issues. If so, that is mild indeed compared with the disarray which has characterized U.S. foreign policy in more recent years.

The mixed picture of performance in the foreign-policy field, combined with the brevity of tenure in office, makes Kennedy's Administration especially frustrating in terms of questions left unanswered. One can be reasonably confident that the more combative side of the President would not have been the dominant feature of a second term in office. Kennedy increasingly looked to the second term as the time for major accomplishment abroad and, especially, at home. The missile crisis was followed in the summer of 1963 by the Partial Nuclear Test-Ban Treaty between the United States and the Soviet Union, under which atmospheric testing of nuclear weapons was banned. The treaty represents a major accomplishment in the efforts to stabilize the arms race and reduce its negative costs. With the passage of time, in fact, the treaty stands out very explicitly as a visible, important milestone in the tortured effort, which in recent years has been rather unsuccessful, to reach arms-control understandings with the Soviets.

Kennedy made the treaty a priority effort, and increasingly during the year he stressed the subjects of peace and disarmament. A speech at American University in June had developed the theme and probably contributed to Soviet flexibility in negotiations. Peace became the motif of a tour of the Western states of the United States which ostensibly was to be devoted to conservation, and in fact was an early venture in the 1964 re-election campaign. No doubt the 'peace issue' would have been featured prominently by Kennedy in the 1964 race, probably in a manner more positive than that used by Lyndon Johnson. The 1963 Western trip was in that sense a prelude. Perhaps Kennedy could have used the approach for positive leverage with both the Europeans and the Soviets. Then suddenly the President was gone.

4 The Global Reach of Great Power

The sudden, shocking transition from John F. Kennedy to Lyndon B. Johnson in the White House inevitably created significant policy ripples reaching far beyond the abrupt change in leadership. American public opinion at all levels was profoundly affected by the assassination of the President. Following the series of shocks to the political nervous system of the United States in the 1960s and early 1970s, including the assassinations of Robert Kennedy and Martin Luther King, the extraordinary divisiveness and bitterness engendered by the Vietnam War, and the scandals of Watergate, Americans have become more cynical and less hopeful about their political environment. Consequently, only with difficulty can one recall the exceptional surprise which greeted the first Kennedy assassination both in the United States and in Europe and the rest of the world.

American history has included a number of attempts, successful and failed, to kill the president. Yet the mythology developed in the twentieth century that this was now a problem of the past. McKinley at the turn of the century had been the last president to be assassinated. If attempts had been made at frequent intervals since that time, the fact that they were unsuccessful obviously bred complacency. The murder of John Kennedy ended that optimistic attitude and also ushered in a period of unpredictable ferment in both domestic and foreign policy.

Kennedy, who in office was reasonably popular but also controversial with his countrymen, was transformed into a hero in death. As we have seen, he had problems with some European leaders but he was generally popular with the public in Europe. His death created a situation in which he became on both sides of the Atlantic a genuine martyr. However serious, or effective, the efforts of some critics to descredit him in more recent years, during the period immediately after his assassination Kennedy was revered as a great leader. Hence, there was no question of major departures from the policy objectives of his New Frontier.

For President Johnson, the requirement to stay tied to past priorities was especially strong in the field of foreign policy. The new president was much more experienced and doubtless more confident in the domestic field, with policy goals congruent with those of Kennedy and the mainstream of the Democratic Party. Kennedy had a genuinely strong interest in foreign policy; Johnson, though sent on various foreign missions during his unhappy tenure as Vice President, was much more comfortable in domestic matters. Throughout his Congressional career, his greatest influence was behind the scenes and, as this implies, he was largely removed from the intense public concern about international events and the position of the country in the competition with the Soviet Union. During the 1960 presidential campaign, he was probably less familiar with the foreign-policy establishment of the United States than any of the leading candidates of either party. Moreover, Kennedy's own record of accomplishment was much thinner in the domestic than in the international arena. In foreign policy, by contrast, Kennedy had seemed increasingly effective. Johnson had less experience and confidence, and the Cold War atmosphere of the time anyway set priorities which he was quite willing to pursue.

In addition, there were the much-commented upon stylistic differences between the two leaders, and this factor perhaps was especially important in the context of European affairs. Kennedy seemed understandable to the West Europeans, and not just those in socially fashionable or intellectual circles. Johnson, in some ways so Amercian, was harder for the Europeans to fathom. Indeed many Europeans viewed him, rightly, as rather alien to them.

For Nato concerns, however, the advent of the new administration was by no means an entirely negative event. Explicitly separating atmosphere from policy helps to make the important point that the Johnson regime was productive in resolving some dilemmas and addressing other aspects of Nato relations in a positive, effective manner. Part of the explanation for this was that Alliance relations to some extent benefitted from less attention on the part of Washington. The Kennedy Administration had pressed a very large number of reforms and initiatives on European allies. Some of these without doubt were important, including notably the effort to rationalize military strategy in the face of a much more threatening Soviet Union.

Some, however, had contained within themselves inherent contradictions and thus problems for relations among the nations. These included the M.L.F. which encapsulated the American inconsistencies in wanting to share power in a collegial manner yet at the same time retain basic control of national strategic nuclear forces. They also included in the view of some the American propensity to promote 'Atlantic partnership' in exceptionally vague terms, with no real surrender of political sovereignty anticipated on the part of Washington. Kennedy also had the comparative luxury of not having to act decisively in terms of choosing among harsh alternatives in these policy matters. As Catherine Kelleher has noted in the course of her thorough study of the subject, 'Kennedy was not forced to make a final decision about the M.L.F. or any other sharing formula'.[1] The same point could also be made about some other difficult policy matters inherited by Johnson. While no decision had yet been forced, the M.L.F. had percolated within the government during the Kennedy years, such that interests had developed commitments to both sides of the issue.

President Johnson was effective in acting reasonably expeditiously to defuse the M.L.F. issue, which had become a source of friction within the Alliance as well as of division in Washington. The unavoidable contradictions involved in the initiative, which in time had become very apparent to Kennedy, could no longer be widely ignored. Working with key officials, Johnson determined to move forcefully and sink the M.L.F. once and for all. Related to this was the downplaying by Washington of the theme of Atlantic partnership. This was not a result of conscious decision because U.S. foreign policy was moving in less ambitious directions, but rather was mainly a function of the new president's primary focus on domestic policy. Also, in international policy terms the country was increasingly preoccupied with South-east Asia, specifically the escalating war in South Vietnam.

The manner in which President Johnson handled the M.L.F. is instructive concerning not only his approach to foreign policy but also the state of Atlantic Alliance relations during that period. The President at first publicly committed himself to the force. During mid-1964, he and the new West German Chancellor, Ludwig Erhard, issued a joint communiqué that stated in part that 'the proposed multilateral force would make a significant addition to this [Atlantic] military and political strength and the efforts should be continued to ready an agreement for signature by the end of the year'.[2] This indicated that, from the perspective of the West German government, the M.L.F. had become of paramount importance to the wider influence and status of the country.

In December 1964, however, with the security and room for manoeuvre provided at least temporarily by a smashing electoral triumph, Johnson was ready to move beyond *pro forma* endorsement of the M.L.F. While continuing to make statements in support of the principle of nuclear sharing, the President also made clear that any arrangements had to reflect the desires of all the major Alliance partners, not just the Americans and West Germans. The British seemed ambivalent on the M.L.F. and the French clearly were opposed to the effort. Johnson was especially forceful in indicating that the door had to be kept open for French involvement, at least at some point in the future.[3]

The many different intragovernmental interests and perspectives within the Administration that seemed to bear on the M.L.F. continued to complicate diplomatic life and, in particular, left many Europeans uneasy. This was particularly true of the West Germans. In Washington, those who gave priority to Alliance cohesion through the new force faced opposition from those more interested in *détente* with the Soviet Union. There were also tensions between M.L.F. advocates, who were mainly concerned to promote non-proliferation of nuclear weapons, and those who were anxious to postpone any more direct confrontations with President de Gaulle.[4]

On the European side was an equally if not more complicated set of factors dragging down the M.L.F. Chancellor Erhard had a large number of domestic political-electoral considerations to worry about, especially in the period leading up to the September 1965 parliamentary elections. The French were becoming increasingly adamant about their refusal to co-operate with American Nato policies. The Soviets were denouncing the M.L.F. in bitter terms. Continuing non-proliferation treaty negotiations led Europeans as well as Americans to criticize a nuclear sharing arrangement which seemed to run counter to the goal of non-proliferation. This led to considerable criticism of the nuclear non-proliferation effort by West Germans, who were anxious to ensure that existing security would not be undermined or future options forestalled by any confrontation or by a Soviet-American accord.

The result of these different influences, not surprisingly, was the ultimate frustration of the M.L.F. initiative. Even after achieving election to the presidency, Johnson initially appeared to be still ambiguous concerning various foreign-policy options. This, however, soon changed. To be fair, Kennedy too had never been very explicit concerning the structure the M.L.F. might assume. In Johnson's case, however, there is the strong impression that scepticism based on instinct was combined with a genuine lack of foreign-policy expertise. In this subject, as on Vietnam, the President's natural decisiveness and drive to control overcame any uncertainty he had on the subject. Johnson moved to veto the plan. The American President could and did live with disorder – indeed, his critics said he encouraged it in foreign policy – but the politician in his nature no doubt recognized the inherent contradictions and lack of balance or trade-offs in the plan.

Johnson brought the long-term project to its end in the context of another major meeting with Erhard. The final communiqué glossed over the problem. However, following this meeting the M.L.F. was dead:

> The President and the Chancellor gave close attention to the nuclear problems confronting the alliance. They agreed that the Federal Republic of Germany and other interested parties in the alliance have an appropriate role in nuclear defense.[5]

The fall of the Erhard government in 1966, combined with the continuing inability of Washington to build a consensus around a specific set of proposals, and of course the President's own opposition, meant that the M.L.F. initiative at long last was removed as a viable policy option. The Grand Coalition which took power in West Germany, combining conservatives and socialists, had different priorities and problems. The M.L.F. would not emerge again as a focus for Alliance debate or speculation about fostering cohesion. Partly to compensate for this experience, the Nuclear Planning Group was established within Nato to co-ordinate such matters, and Germany was a regular member. Thus, even though the plan which had absorbed American attention was defeated, the long-term goal of integration of the Federal Republic into the Western Alliance was furthered. For the State Department, however, the result was a setback in terms of the competition for influence and standing within the American government.[6]

U.S.–SOVIET RELATIONS

The ultimate defeat of the M.L.F. reflected not only the increasingly obvious inherent contradiction in the proposal from the viewpoints of both Washington and Nato, to say nothing of the attitudes of capitals in other Nato nations, but also the growing perception that there were possibilities for genuine *détente* with the Soviet Union. This appeared to be a much more promising possibility as the 1960s reached their mid-point. The long-term crisis over Berlin had not disappeared but had cooled considerably. The Partial Nuclear Test-Ban Treaty between the United States and the Soviet Union represented a major diplomatic triumph and was therefore stabilizing in both important symbolic and practical ways. Finally, as noted earlier, arguably the very fact that the Johnson Administration was not so preoccupied with Atlantic-area relations meant that there would be less likelihood of a direct clash. Lack of attention made conflict less apparent or substantial within the Alliance. American foreign-policy attention and energies as the decade wore on were much more directed toward other parts of the world, beyond Europe, than had been the case previously.

The combination of American preoccupation elsewhere and apparent Soviet restraint meant that pressures for the sort of Atlantic defence collaboration that brought forth the M.L.F. became much less significant. The Johnson Administration gave domestic reform legislation a very high priority, in many ways the highest since New Deal days. Certainly the President was more effective in moving a large amount of legislation through Congress than any of his predecessors since Franklin Roosevelt. The Vietnam War was by 1965 a major preoccupation, and other foreign-policy considerations were more and more crowded out. Concerning the Soviets, we know now that a very substantial, continuing, indeed relentless military build-up commenced in the early 1960s. This reality was not clear until later, however. What was more visible at the time were the tentative steps toward accommodation between the superpowers following the 1962 Cuban missile crisis, the tangible accomplishment of the 1963 Partial Nuclear Test-Ban Treaty, and the more stable – if less colourful – demeanour of Soviet foreign policy after the ousting of Krushchev in 1964.[7] All of these elements considered together, however, meant that the international system from the viewpoint of Washington was moving away from the Atlanticism that had earlier been such a heavy focus of U.S. foreign policy. One source argues,

> from Roosevelt's time through the Kennedy administration, the American establishment tended to regard the Atlantic or the European theaters as decisive as far as American interests were

concerned. Orthodox Marxism, and Stalinist practitioners during the 1930's, the 1940's, and the 1950's, had been principally focused upon the central theater also.[8]

Incipient Soviet-American *détente,* however, added to the increasingly global focus and non-European preoccupation of U.S. foreign policy to draw attention away from the Atlantic area.

The waning of an immediate, direct focus by the United States and the Soviet Union, and their Nato and Warsaw Pact associates, on the Central European confrontation provided an opportunity for diplomatic initiatives on the part of other European states. France, West Germany and Britain all engaged in significant moves during this time, and arguably the first two were responding to an environment more conducive to taking risks and exercising imagination. This was mainly possible because the Americans were less attentive to events. The British largely continued with the gradual withdrawal into Europe that had already begun after the Second World War. The point can be made that they perhaps benefitted from an absence of the temptations to play great-power mediator between the two superpowers, an effort that had been so important to Prime Minister Macmillan. Otherwise, however, they did not so much act as react to encroaching international circumstances. This was not the case with the French and Germans, who moved respectively against American domination of Atlantic-area affairs and toward accommodation with the Soviet Union. In the former case there was partial, and in the latter considerable, success in the endeavour.

FRANCE AND NATO

The most striking move by Paris in the offensive against the American – or in de Gaulle's phrase the 'Anglo-Saxon' – leadership of the Alliance was forcing Nato headquarters out of France, and the wider related removal of French forces from Nato command. President de Gaulle laid out French national policy in this field in a letter to President Johnson of 7 March 1966. He developed therein the thesis that France would remain part of the security understanding in broad terms, while withdrawing from specific institutional co-operation. After restating French commitment to the common defence, de Gaulle continued,

France considers that the changes which have taken place since 1949, or are now taking place, in Europe, Asia and elsewhere, as well as the development of her situation, do not justify, as far as she is concerned, the arrangements of a military nature made after the conclusion of the Alliance either in common in the form of multilateral conventions or by special agreements between the French and the American governments.

This is why France is determined to regain on her whole territory the full exercise of her sovereignty, at present diminished by the permanent presence of Allied military elements or by the use which is made of her air space; to cease her participation in the integrated Commands; and no longer to place her forces at the disposal of Nato[9]

The French move left the Americans and the rest of the Nato allies no choice but to move the headquarters of the Alliance from Paris. Brussels was chosen as the new location for Nato facilities. Yet if the French demand could not be ignored or denied, the Johnson Administration did not have to accept the new state of affairs in silence. The U.S. President in fact complained very directly in his response to de Gaulle,

I am puzzled by your view that the presence of Allied military forces on French soil impairs the sovereignty of France. These forces have been there at French invitation pursuant to a common plan to help ensure the security of France and her allies.[10]

Once more the leadership of France, though heading a nation technically less powerful than the United States in economic and military terms, and indeed by no means the dominant nation in Europe, had enjoyed a significant political victory. There were several major underlying reasons for this. First, the French President, who may have seemed quite quixotic to Washington and other capitals, in fact selected his terrain for conflict with considerable care. He usually limited creation of serious crises to areas which were central to the continued health and survival of the state, such as liquidation of the frustrating war in Algeria, or where the possibilities were very good that he could totally control the tempo and outcome. Forcing Nato headquarters out of Paris and the veto on British entry into the European Common Market fall in this latter category.

Second, de Gaulle appreciated the importance of moving very quickly in order to gain maximum surprise. He was a master at not revealing his moves before he had made them. This applies not only to such sudden shocks as his Nato and Common Market moves, but also to the public impact of comparatively complex and long-planned events, including the 1963 Franco-German treaty. The removal of Nato facilities from Paris, and concomitant withdrawal of France from the Alliance command and control structure, was handled in such a way that virtually all the other nations involved were taken by surprise.

Third, if Nato partners were hardly happy with the French move, the President gained considerably at home through demonstraion of national independence, and that of course was the principal incentive for his actions. He was able to achieve maximum impact on domestic opinion precisely because the decision was so startling. French independence from American control involved both image and reality – indeed, the imagery involved was the primary reason for de Gaulle's initiative. The move complicated and frustrated Nato's operation but hardly did irreparable harm to the structure, and arguably permanent damage was never the French goal.

What struck many outside observers as irritating, if not petty, was however very central to the French strategy of dramatic self-assertion. President Johnson's stated puzzlement about the reason for it is understandable; equally understandable was the need of the French to show they could participate in a security pact without sacrificing basic control over their own national military force. This was also, of course, a way to demonstrate that Washington was no longer as much in charge as before, that there were ways to combine alliance with separation, and that the world of Atlantic affairs was considerably more complex that the simple imagery of two nuclear superpowers might suggest.

De Gaulle also pursued independence on the economic front, further demonstrating that the world of the 1960s was far different from that of the 1950s. Among those who have analysed this period, Alfred Grosser has pointed out with particular insight and skill that the 1960s witnessed increasing European concern about American domination even as the American economic position was growing more insecure. Indeed, the roots of independence, stimulated by economic recovery from the effects of the Second World War, are reflected in European chafing at American control. There was concern about the encroachment of American popular culture and styles along with worry about domination by American corporations.

The spread of fashions and eating habits, of entertainment styles (dance, music, songs, movies, television, and of certain methods of management) went hand in hand with a feeling of domination which had to be denounced all the more vigorously as it had the characteristics of foreign rule.[11]

The most prominent voice sounding the alarm about American influence in Western Europe was Jean-Jacques Servan-Schreiber, whose book *The American Challenge* quickly became a best-seller on both sides of the Atlantic after publication in 1968. There is a curiously dated quality about these arguments now, when the Americans are locked in ruthless economic competition with the Japanese and face, too, serious challenges in various market areas from the Europeans, especially the French and Germans. Servan-Schreiber observed in his book, 'Fifteen years from now it is quite possible that the world's greatest industrial power, just after the United States and Russia, will not be Europe, but American industry in Europe.'[12]

De Gaulle had a very useful source of leverage over the Americans thanks to the increasingly serious currency pressure and strains of the period. Although not generally recognized at the time, especially in Washington, these years were the beginning of the breakdown of the Bretton Woods system for international economic mangement, primarily but not exclusively among the advanced industrial nations. The inflation generated by the manner in which the Administration handled the financing of the Vietnam War, through large deficits rather than higher taxes, created even more problems. Europeans resented the fact that U.S. inflation was being exported and that they were compelled to finance the American military effort through the indirect tax of the inflation. They experienced both a cheapening of the value of their own dollar-holdings and, later, inflation in their own domestic price system.

The quite substantial Eurodollar supplies themselves reflected and were a source of difficulties. When the American Federal Reserve Board tried to tighten monetary policy in the face of the inflationary fiscal deficits of the Johnson Administration, dollars in Europe were deployed to frustrate this policy, a result not at all surprising given both the size of the holdings and the rise which occurred in U.S. interest rates. The Eurodollar supplies reflected directly the continuing U.S. negative balance of payments with Europe. These deficits in turn drew attention to the very large numbers of American troops stationed in

Europe. This was an important factor in the deficits, and pressures on West Germany to do more to offset the burden were a continuing issue in relations with the Americans and also with the British.[13]

De Gaulle meanwhile tried to force a devaluation of the U.S. dollar in *de facto* terms by bringing about an increase in the price of gold. While not formally committed to a gold standard, the French President on occasion had defended the importance of a fixed gold standard and criticized the Americans for handling the burden of overcommitment and multiple ambitions through the expedient of printing more money. During his last six months in office, he was actively engaged in trying to bring this about. France had withdrawn from the existing European gold pool, which had been created primarily to stabilize the price, and was independently buying gold in order to effect a price increase through scarcity.[14]

The very fact that de Gaulle was able to operate in this way, causing considerable concern in Washington and for that matter other European capitals, was an indication of a broader fundamental fact of international life – namely, that the era of American dominance was over and that the Europeans had to interact with their now more equal superpower ally in an effort to create a new set of relationships and arrangements. This was the reality whether or not de Gaulle succeeded in his national ambitions. Several steps were taken in this direction between the initiation of de Gaulle's direct pressure and the Nixon economic shocks of 1971. Most apparent was the need to address the problem of lack of liquidity despite the very large Eurodollar deposits. The world economy had simply grown too large to be covered in formal terms through the existing gold standard. Consequently, S.D.R.s – Special Drawing Rights – were created to increase available funds. This amounted to a new form of currency, not backed directly by gold but the value of which would be recognized by all countries. France was ultimately brought into this system in 1969, after de Gaulle had left the presidency, by his successor Georges Pompidou.

Another move taken in concert was to remove the gold market from influence on government currency rates. The commercial market was opened so that prices could fluctuate but this would normally have no effect on government gold prices. The strains indicated that the post-war system was changing and to some extent coming apart, yet the Atlantic-area nations were demonstrating a capacity to co-operate in framing new mechanisms to address the situation. The industrialized countries were able to look to options beyond simply retreating into isolationism and beggar-thy-neighbour policies. Most significant of all, the Americans did not respond to the French challenge in a way that would worsen Atlantic relations. There was a serious debate within Congress over possible reduction in the number of forces in Western Europe, yet the Americans ultimately decided to retain the ties to Europe, at least by implication, as legislative pressure for withdrawal waned.

The question of the effectiveness and wisdom of de Gaulle's basic foreign policy leads to a more complex, ambiguous answer. There was a tone of prejudice and vindictiveness at times in his remarks about the Americans and the British which implies hostility simply for the sake of hostility. Despite his subtlety, the approach seemed too directly reminiscent of the classic balance-of-power system, even though the nuclear military and other capacities of the superpower – heavily military in the case of the Soviet Union, economic as well in the case of the United States, scientific and technological in both – inevitably place the two in a political and strategic category by themselves.

Yet there were also clearly positive dimensions to de Gaulle's presence and policies concerning effective co-operation in the Atlantic realm. As Stanley Hoffmann has often pointed out, de Gaulle frequently articulated sentiments which were held in European capitals which had less colourful and daring leaders. The French were not alone in bridling at the dominance of the Alliance by Washington. De Gaulle, many times accused of irrational animus toward the European Community, also in fact represented broader scepticism about the real potential for supranational political integration. He was rightly accused of sparking a great Community crisis in 1965–6 by refusing to grant the Commission of the Community independent financial and hence political authority. The French walked out of the Council of the Community, thus halting business, including any progress in building a stronger supranational political as well as administrative structure. They returned some months later only when the proposals for independent financial levies for the Commission, and majority rule on policy decisions without veto by single members, had been abandoned. Less publicized at that time or since was the fact that none of the six members of the Community, including the generally pro-integration Dutch, was really in favour of the package put forward by the Commission. The French walk-out from the Council of Ministers was dramatic and unified the remaining five in opposition to that action, but this masked the fact that there was considerable agreement with the thrust of French objections. None of the members of the Community really wanted to give national sovereignty away to supranational institutions in crucial areas of financial control or open the door to loss of decision-making power in such fundamental realms as economic or security policies.[15]

Also, de Gaulle was accurate in underlining the continuing importance of the nation state and highlighting the ambiguities and inconsistencies in Washington policies. The Americans spoke of an emerging Atlantic community of nations yet were never very clear or specific about how and in what terms national independence would be moved to supranational authority. The M.L.F. was described as a sharing arrangement, yet the thrust of Washington attitudes on flexible response was to centralize as much control as possible over nuclear weapons in American hands. Washington in effect wanted to have it both ways; visions of co-operation and democratic decision-making, but a reality of control and leadership by the power which was dominant economically as well as militarily. De Gaulle clarified these inconsistencies, drew attention to them, provoked thought as well as controversy about them, while at the same time carrying out the not inconsiderable tasks of creating political stability and institutional legitimacy in his own country.[16]

GERMANY

If de Gaulle managed national self-definition through conflict with the main Alliance partner in the West, Willy Brandt carried out national renewal through accommodation with his principal adversaries in the East. In 1969, the leaders of the Social Democratic Party in West Germany for the first time moved to national governmental power in their own right, without the need for coalition with another party. This in itself represented a milestone in the development and ratification of democratic political culture and practices in the Federal Republic. Also involved, of course, was the strong national mandate for Brandt to operate effectively to bring about significant adjustments in the relationship with the East. This was the start of profoundly significant, ultimately successful shifts in West German diplomacy designed to normalize relations with the Eastern bloc states. Election of the Social Democrats was also, however, the culmination of a process of movement toward true competitive party democracy for which Adenauer had set the stage over a period of years. The success of the socialists in peaceful transition was perhaps the most important testament to Adenauer's greatness, an ironic development which some Christian

Democrats – though not all – would have welcomed.

Willy Brandt's diplomatic success also reflected a series of more tentative, less successful steps taken by earlier West German government leaders. Adenauer, true to his Cold War sentiments, eager for good relations with the Eisenhower Administration and especially his friend John Foster Dulles, and conscious of the need to build a German identity and allay Western worries about accommodation with the Soviets, was not anxious to create new ties with Eastern regimes. His foreign minister, Gerhard Schröder, however, did take some tentative steps, generally in the area of trade relations. He worked to create agreements without technically contravening the Hallstein Doctrine, which held that there would be no recognition by Bonn of states that had formal relations with the German Democratic Republic. Schröder was able to achieve trade treaties in 1963 with Hungary, Poland and Romania, and in 1964 with Bulgaria. His only real failure in this limited effert was with Czechoslovakia. De Gaulle in France, busy with his own moves toward Moscow, was generally supportive of German efforts along this line, especially since he was trying to encourage independence from Washington on the part of Bonn.

Adenauer became more sympathetic to such steps thanks to his growing irritation with the Kennedy Administration. Many of the sources of tension were stylistic, relating to different personalities and indeed generations then in power in the United States. This was compounded by substantive problems, including European suspicion of American emphasis on flexible response. In any case, just as Adenauer found new reasons to be friendly with de Gaulle in the West, so did he not oppose efforts of his deputy to create new linkages in the East, or at least he did not rule these initiatives out completely. Any misgivings were well controlled.

In many ways, although not as successful as those who came later, Schröder is especially to be admired by those who favour stabilization and *détente* in Central Europe. He bore the domestic criticisms of those who felt these steps were somehow in important ways legitimizing Soviet domination, even while concern was growing in the Soviet Union that German efforts would undermine the tight control over satellites previously exercised. There was more understandable Communist worry that the East German regime might be isolated by Bonn, which was concentrating attention elsewhere in Eastern Europe.[17]

Turbulence in both West Germany and the Soviet Union in leadership circles prevented Schröder from moving even more ambitiously.

He was only starting to approach Moscow directly about new accords when Khrushchev was abruptly ousted in 1964, thus ending possibilities there for the immediate future. Adenauer's successor, Ludwig Erhard, had given Schröder considerable leeway to pursue his initiatives, which were in turn bolstered by the new chancellor's more positive attitude. Adenauer had been accepting but largely grudging; Erhard was much more open and interested. Erhard suffered, however, from a variety of domestic and foreign-policy difficulties throughout his tenure. His departure from office in 1966 further complicated opportunities for an orderly, effective *Ostpolitik*.[18] Overshadowed by both his predecessor and his Social Democratic successor, he was robbed of the major place in European diplomatic history which his early intellectual accomplishments and long-term political loyalty seemed to promise.

The Erhard government was followed by the 'Grand Coalition' of the Christian Democratic and Christian Social Unions in combination with the Social Democrats. The regime in retrospect had certain strengths and advantages. These included the breadth of representation, which smoothed the way toward the ultimate move of the Social Democrats directly into governmental power on their own, in turn confirming the legitimacy of the West German democratic political system. There was also the somewhat complementary combination of political talents of Chancellor Kurt Kiesinger and Foreign Minister Willy Brandt.

The Grand Coalition provided the ultimate legitimacy for the concept of opening new relations with the East, at least at the start. This was encouraged by similar interest in U.S. foreign-policy circles, which were not yet totally preoccupied with the Vietnam War. President Johnson made a major speech in 1966 urging 'the idea of building bridges to all the Eastern European countries'. In the same year Zbigniew Brzezinski, who was joining Johnson's and Secretary of State Dean Rusk's policy-planning staff in the State Department, published a book which developed in detail the argument that new relationships could be worked out with the Communist-bloc states. The government in Bonn began to sound similar themes, although the Social Democrats were considerably more enthusiastic about such prospects than were their more conservative partners, including in particular Chancellor Kiesinger. The Chancellor was at most ambiguous, and tensions grew with Brandt over time. Kiesinger did explicitly call for 'a German contribution to the maintenance of peace', declaring without qualification that this was the prime goal of the government in the international arena. There were revived efforts to establish rapport with the Soviet Union, including accords on 'renunciation of force'. High priority was given to diplomatic relations with both Czechoslovakia and Poland.

The main stumbling-block within the coalition was how to relate to the German Democratic Republic. On the one hand, the West Germans were quite willing to include the other state in the more general accommodation. On the other hand, Kiesinger had problems with anything approaching regular diplomatic recognition. He stressed non-political contacts, including educational and cultural dimensions, 'so that the two parts of our people do not become strangers to each other during their separation'.[19]

The new coalition enjoyed some successes in policy initiatives toward the Eastern bloc. Diplomatic relations with Romania were established quickly, thanks to considerable preliminary work by the previous Erhard government. The earlier complexity provided by the problems of which Germany to recognize was simply ignored, thus rendering the Hallstein Doctrine, which had dominated Bonn's foreign policy, immediately a dead letter. Kiesinger and Brandt also shrewdly met with de Gaulle, after which they talked of closer co-ordination of foreign policy between the two countries. Thus they removed the looming danger which had been represented by supporters of de Gaulle in West Germany who had been chary of the initiatives toward the East.[20]

These successes were, however, rather short-lived. After normalizing relations with the independent Romania, and the even more distinctive regime in Yugoslavia, the West German government began to lose momentum in the effort to open Eastern doors. Moreover, pressure started to grow from both Washington and Moscow to sign the Nuclear Non-Proliferation Treaty. This provided a fresh complication to Alliance relations of the sort that heartened Gaullists in both France and Gemany. The treaty was criticized by them as yet another example of superpower collusion at the expense of the middle powers. The fact that the accord would prevent even peaceful uses of atomic energy, according to critics, was an important practical reason for opposition.[21]

The partnership of Brandt and Kiesinger was not without strains, and there were certain important advantages for West German foreign policy when the 1969 parliamentary elections brought a clear majority for the Soviet Democratic Party. Brandt then took over as chancellor in his own right, without the need to compromise with the conservative wing of the Grand Coalition. Kiesinger's Nazi background during the Second World War had complicated life for the government after the information had become public knowledge. Moreover, the inter-personal and policy relationship between the two leaders and their supporters had begun to change for the worse. No doubt this was the result in part of naturally developing frictions over time between two very strong personalities.

There were more specific policy disputes. Kiesinger was rather strongly interested in the maintenance of a European nuclear option, very likely in the context of closer Franco-German co-operation. Brandt's own priorities were much more in the direction of emphasis on possibilities for nuclear non-proliferation accord, even if that pre-cluded a West German nuclear role. Brandt was most probably the better representative of public opinion on this and other policy issues. There was also the point that the Christian Democrats had been in power for a very long time, and a natural evolution toward an alterna-tive government had been in progress for several years.[22]

In the parliamentary elections of September 1969, Brandt was elected along with the rest of his party to a majority position in the *Bundestag*. He became a prominent and popular leader not only in his own country but also in Western Europe and the Atlantic area more generally. The liberal Free Democrats became coalition partners with the Social Democrats, and that party's leader, Walter Scheel, was selected as foreign minister in the new government.

The prospect which confronted Brandt was in many ways daunting, though there were clear compensations in being the head of a socialist government at last. The previous two years had witnessed a gradual loss of momentum in the movement toward the East – *Ostpolitik* – following initial successes, and this frustrating situation was not to be changed through the shift in government parties alone. Although the East German regime indicated some flexibility on particular issues, including such matters as postal and traffic rules, the East Germans essentially were hostile to any changes in the *status quo*. They demanded, among other things, that Bonn drop out of both Nato and the European Community if reconciliation between the two parts of Germany was to be achieved. This was clearly an impossible demand. The two conditions led the Christian Democrats when in the Grand Coalition to resist any further co-operation with the East.

There was also a more general deterioration of relations. Near the end of 1967, the Soviets and East Germans began to renew pressure against West Berlin. The East Germans prohibited West German government officials from meeting in West Berlin, which represented violation of a basic right in Western eyes. Also, passport and visa problems, and other complications, began to arise once again to delay and otherwise complicate travel from West Germany to West Berlin. Again, this represented a marked change from the recent pattern of East German behaviour. The most serious complication by far for *Ostpolitik,* however, was the Soviet invasion of Czechoslovakia in 1968.[23] This ended not only prospects for fresh understandings between Eastern and Western Europe, but also brought to an abrupt halt Soviet and American Strategic Arms Limitation Talks (Salt) which had been planned following the successful Glassboro summit.

Despite the difficulty of the challenge, Brandt was able to move relatively quickly and effectively, especially in view of earlier frustrations and growing Soviet–American tension, to establish relations with major Eastern powers. Thanks to his governement's efforts, the post-Second World War *status quo* in Eastern and Central Europe was stabilized and rationalized. Even before the federal elections, as noted, Kiesinger and the Christian Democrats had been working away from endorsement of *Ostpolitik* while the Free Democrats had moved closer to Brandt. This helped to break the Grand Coalition, but also meant that once in power Brandt had considerable freedom of manoeuvre, at least for a time. In mid-August 1970, the West Germans signed an important Renunciation of Force Treaty with the Soviet Union. After long, very tortured negotiations, including setbacks that seemed to reflect East European even more than Soviet intransigence, a fundamental normalization of the status of Berlin was achieved in 1972.

This was a function of important changes in the larger international political stage, including support for *détente* by the Nixon Administration and the fluid environment in arms-control negotiations, encompassing both Salt and the Mutual Balanced Force Reduction (M.B.F.R.) talks. Brandt also achieved important accords with Poland in 1970, including acceptance of the Oder–Neisse line as the border. There was a major treaty with Czechoslovakia in 1973. Thus each of the major tension areas remaining from the Second World War had been accommodated.[24]

BRITAIN

The situation of the British was quite different, as indicated, but there were also some major developments during this period in terms of their relationship with both the United States and important European allies. Often these took place in the context of events overseas in the Commonwealth and the lingering remnants of empire. The most important, however, was the British success at long last in entering the European Common Market. This demonstrated that Britain was finally focused explicitly, without further illusion or self-deception, on Europe. It also signified that the West Europeans, including in particular the French, were willing to welcome them at last into the Community fold.

The former shift was the most significant, masked in part by years of French intransigence regarding institutional participation in the European supranational effort. Retreat is rarely heroic, and partly for this reason British foreign policy since the Second World War has often been criticized, sometimes very caustically, for lack of foresight in recognition of the need to abandon empire, to emphasize the Commonwealth less, and focus on the requirements of involvement in Europe. Movement from the status of great power to that of clearly a middle-ranked power was difficult. Yet, if retreat is rarely heroic, and is sometimes traumatic, the British did demonstrate that they could handle such a major transition smoothly and with a minimal amount of domestic instability as a result. As late as Harold Macmillan's tenure as Prime Minister in the early 1960s, the British leadership were fond of viewing their nation as roughly on a par with the two superpowers. By the end of the decade, Harold Wilson could no longer credibly claim the same role.

The British experienced continuity in their strong partnership with Washington in the shift from the Eisenhower to the Kennedy Administration, as discussed earlier. Again, this represented a major contrast with the French and German cases, where relations measurably declined. Unfortunately, the same situation did not occur in the transition from the Kennedy to Johnson. Perhaps this was because the Anglophilia of the assassinated American President and his chief officials was pronounced; perhaps a conservative West German regime was somewhat more easily able to accommodate the new tone and interests in American foreign policy. In any case, the remainder of the 1960s and the early 1970s witnessed a gradual separation between the United States and Britain, a waning of the significance of the special relationship.

There was by no means, however, an entirely negative tone to the Anglo-American relationship during this period, and again the M.L.F. experience becomes instructive. The British characteristically took their own initiative to try to generate positive movement in military co-operation among Atlantic-area nations. If they did not break the barriers or cut through the Gordian Knot of technical disagreements, they did at least demonstrate support for integration and distract attention somewhat from the ultimate American decision to abandon the M.L.F. idea. Dubbed the 'Thorneycroft proposals', the British initiative involved a much larger combination of types of weapon and clearly moved away from emphasis on naval force. The specific proposal was to put together a force to include British Canberra, American and German F-104 Starfighters, Pershing missiles in Europe, and several other British and American planes. Individual aircraft would retain national crews, but units would comprise participants from different Nato nations.

There was a self-serving quality to the proposals, because the British would be keeping the independence of their Polaris submarine nuclear force, but there were other advantages as well. In practical terms, mixed manning would probably work better in the context of aircraft and missile units, with particular units retaining their integrity. Also, there would be no need to establish a new force, since existing weapons and men could be employed.[25]

The accession to power of the Labour Party as a result of the 1964 general election represented a major solidification, not change, in the direction of British Alliance policy. This was ironic, since Harold Wilson, the new prime minister, had been a leader of the left wing of the party. Moreover, nuclear-weapons issues had been a source of the most intense, emotional division within the Labour Party and indeed the British population more generally in the years immediately preceding the electoral victory. Finally, the Labour Party had been clear in opposition to entry into the European Common Market; instinctive socialist isolationism combined with suspicion of an institutional structure which promoted unity on a basis other than class lines.

Given this prelude, Wilson, showing his characteristic policy agility, moved to reinforce British commitments, both tangible and abstract, to both the Alliance and Europe. The Labour Party had been very critical of the M.L.F., as indeed had the Conservatives. Rather than oppose the American initiative head-on, however, the new government followed the Tory lead in advocating a different sort of multilateral force. As with the Conservative proposal, the force would be clearly under Nato command and would contain a larger number of different weapons components. This time, however, the Polaris submarine fleet was included, as indeed would be at least an equal number of U.S. nuclear submarines. Not only was Wilson coming down on the side of the Alliance, but in technical terms he also could argue to the Labour left wing that the new government was demonstrating opposition to the Nassau accords and to the principle of a truly independent British nuclear deterrent.[26]

The British proposal for an Atlantic Nuclear Force also paid some dividends in terms of the relationship with the United States. There was understandable concern in London that the initiative might not only complicate relations with the most important ally, but actually result in serious tensions and disagreements. In the event, however, President Johnson appeared to welcome the British suggestions, perhaps because by then he had decided in his own mind that the M.L.F. was simply not a viable Alliance policy. Johnson and Wilson met in Washington in early December 1964 and apparently quickly agreed on the impracticality of the M.L.F. notion, however constructed. Although Johnson had taken some peripheral interest in the force issue during his term as Vice President, he did not really become engaged in the complex details until he succeeded to the presidency. He apparently spent a great deal of time preparing himself for the meeting with Wilson, a process which led to increasing scepticism about the force. In this reaction, he was not unlike Kennedy. Johnson, however, had by the end of 1964 been returned to office with an enormous popular and electoral-college majority, providing freedom to act decisively on the international stage as well as move forward an ambitious legislative programme at home.

The President was probably conscious of Soviet hostility, growing divisions were emerging in West Germany, the French clearly were antagonistic on this matter as on others, and other European allies were not positive about the approach. The fact that even the British were not in favour of the basic American proposals no doubt gave pause to the President, though London also probably exaggerated the influence of the Labour government's attitudes on the final decision by Johnson. The concept of a 'special relationship' continued to imply something resembling equality from the British point of view.[27] Finally, of course, opposition to the force was growing in the U.S. Congress.

Harold Wilson did begin to move the country in new directions in policy. To some extent, he was trying to establish a different identity for his new Labour government. This was, after all, a period when socialist party and government rhetoric was filled with references to modernization, progress and in some sense 'getting Britain moving again'. If he was successful in muting the traditional class war and industrial nationalization aspects of the Labour Party, no mean accomplishment for a man who had recently led the left, he was also adept at portraying his party as one of movement compared to the stale and tired Tory regime which had governed for so long. He tried to articulate the changing relationship in his speech during the Washington visit:

> We regard our relationship with you not as a *special relationship* but as a *close relationship,* governed by the only things that matter, unity of purpose and unity in our objectives. We don't come to you at any time on the basis of our past grandeur or any faded thought of what grandeur was . . . . We have, and we always will have, a close relationship.[28]

Unfortunately, while the Atlantic Nuclear Force was of some service to Johnson in his scuttling of the M.L.F., and the initial meetings between the two leaders went well, the Vietnam War soon emerged as a basic source of discord in the Anglo-American relationship. This was true to some extent of the relationship with the European allies generally, but in the case of Britain the sense of betrayal on the part of hardliners in Washington was especially great. Wilson apparently consistently urged that the Americans should not become any more directly engaged in the quagmire of South-east Asia. Aside from the fact that the traditional relationship (whether 'special' or 'close') meant that the Americans reacted with special irritation to what was seen by them as a lack of support, the British were in the mid-1960s engaged in a roughly similar exercise in Malaysia, following very effective counter-insurgency warfare in Malaya in earlier years. The fact that the Vietnam War was divisive in the United States, a point which justified British reticence, could only reinforce Administration irritation with the ally.

Lingering sentiments about the special relationship, combined with Britain's history of involvement in Asia, no doubt fuelled the intensity of the Johnson Administration's reaction to the lack of support demonstrated for the escalation in Vietnam. Secretary of State Dean Rusk, with obvious anger, at one point drew direct parallels between the defence of South-east Asia, specifically the government of South Vietnam, and the defence of Europe against Hitler during the Second World War, noting that the Europeans could forget about receiving such help from the Americans in any future conflict. In more specific terms, he told Louis Heren, the highly sympathetic British journalist, 'All we needed was one regiment: the Black Watch would have done. But you would not. Well don't expect us to save you again. They can invade Sussex and we wouldn't do a damn thing about it.'[29]

President Johnson made clear that even a token, symbolic British military contribution would be sufficient, and he reacted with anger when Wilson not only did not provide the troops but also attempted to mediate and otherwise urge restraint. The Prime Minister became much more specific in urging American caution as military escalation in Vietnam began in earnest from early 1965. Unfortunately, the main result was to alienate and antagonize the American President, with evidence provided by occasional outbursts of the famous Johnson temper. Wilson in his memoirs outlines his serious sense of failure at not having an impact on the diplomacy – or lack thereof – that characterized American policy in Vietnam. In February 1965, Wilson was rebuffed when he telephoned Johnson to express concern over the escalating war. The President said in part, 'if you want to help us some in Vietnam, send us some men and send us some folks to deal with these guerrillas. And announce in the press that you are going to help us'. In June 1966, Wilson's declared opposition to bombing Hanoi and Haiphong was followed by escalation precisely in that manner on those targets.[30]

The most significant British diplomatic initiative concerning the war ended in disappointment and embarrassment for the Prime Minister. In February 1967, Wilson, with some encouragement from Washington, took advantage of Soviet Prime Minister Kosygin's visit to London to present suggestions for de-escalation by both sides in Vietnam – a slowdown of the air war over the North, to be followed by a reduction in levels of ground combat by the two sides. The effort not only was in line with Britain's historic role as international mediator: it was also apt in that Britain and the Soviet Union had jointly chaired the 1954 Geneva conference which had resulted in the partition of Vietnam. Unfortunately, Wilson's specific proposals were not acceptable to Johnson, apparently because too much time would elapse between the first and second phases of the de-escalation. At least, this was the explanation forthcoming from Washington.

After thinking success was in hand, and acting accordingly in dealing with very senior Soviet visitors, the Wilson government was at the very last moment compelled to withdraw the initiative. The failure of effective communication between the Americans and the British was painful for both sides, but much more so for the latter, because humiliation was included. The episode illustrated different things, including the U.S. President's fixation on details, his unpredictability, Washington's concentration on technical specifics rather than wider war goals, and, of course, the British desire to have an impact on superpower relations and wars in distant places as evidence of continued great-power status. The ultimate result, however, was to underscore British dependence on, and in this case also lack of rapport with, the Americans. In effect, not great-power status but the reverse was demonstrated.[31]

Harold Wilson's failure to have any detectable effect on the American military adventure in South-east Asia, except in provoking adverse reactions from the beleaguered Johnson Administration, brought home the point that Britain could not any longer assume great-power status. This was especially the case with an American president who was highly suspicious of both the U.S. Eastern establishment and the British ties which had been so important to that Anglophile group.

One reason, though by no means the only one, for lack of British influence was the continued reduction in national military capabilities. The gradual contraction of forces around the world, begun after the Second World War, continued through the 1960s. Defence Secretary Denis Healey in the Wilson government carried out yet another in a series of military-policy reviews. As usual, no dramatic changes were proposed. A variety of specific cuts in forces was outlined and, for the most part, carried out. These reductions in turn served further to antagonize the Americans, who were urging just the reverse direction in British policy. The army was cut back from a total strength of 180,000 to approximately 165,000. The entire aircraft carrier force was to be taken out of service by 1975, which in turn implied reductions in the air force. Ultimately the carrier decision was delayed, yet the report does indicate awareness that the British role in the world was changing. Forces departed from Aden, Singapore and even Malaysia.

British attitudes on intervention followed those dictates of military reality. There were explicit statements to the effect that the British would not become involved in local brushfire wars where they lacked either important allied backing or the support of the government and population of the afflicted area. Thus acceptance of the reduction in international power was combined with an appreciation of the policy implications of the end of empire. Economic realities were drawing the British toward Europe at the same time as military realities were pushing them toward that regional role.[32]

Wilson's tenure was also significant for the second major initiative for entry into the European Community. After a past as leader of the left wing of the party, he was instrumental in bringing Labour around to acceptance of British entry. Once again, his great policy flexibility, combined with agility in getting policy change more widely accepted, was demonstrated. A second application for membership was put forward. De Gaulle in 1967 again vetoed the British initiative. Nevertheless, Wilson's effort solidified, at least for the time being, entry into the Common Market as a fundamental and also bipartisan national goal.

The final years of 1960s witnessed important Nato steps which either clarified or dismissed policy tangles which had become significant within the Alliance. In 1967 the Nato nations adopted at long last 'flexible response' as formal policy. At the same time, the Nuclear Planning Group was set up to integrate the allied nations more effectively on questions of nuclear policy. This was also the period of the Harmel Report, issued at the end of 1967, which defined 'progress toward a more stable relationship' with the Eastern bloc as a major Alliance goal.[33]

This was a time of new currents in the international political atmosphere, including elements of what would later commonly be termed *détente*. Thus, the long years of the intense Soviet–American Cold War were beginning to draw to a close. The Johnson–Kosygin summit meeting at Glassboro, New Jersey, though inconclusive in its immediate effects (much to the relief of U.S. presidential candidate Richard Nixon), did represent the first direct steps towards the Salt treaties. The Soviet suppression of free political expression and debate in Czechoslovakia also put an end to any immediate prospects for arms accords between the two sides. Yet, despite these setbacks, a more fluid and opportune, less predictable diplomatic environment was in the making.[34]

In early 1969, the Johnson Administration, successful in the conventional political criteria of domestic policy legislation, nevertheless came to an end with an aura of profound spiritual defeat. The Vietnam War, which the President had been so determined to prosecute, increasingly with purely conventional means as more exotic alternatives failed, ultimately defeated him. The Tet Offensive of early 1968 may have been a military victory for the Americans and their South Vietnamese allies in technical military terms. The political impact, however, was quite the reverse. Coming on the heels of extraordinarily optimistic predictions of victory by Johnson, Defense Secretary Robert McNamara and General William Westmoreland, the Viet

Cong attacks were perfectly timed and executed for the desired impact on American public opinion.

THE NIXON YEARS

Thanks to this picture of the departing Johnson Administration, the new Nixon Administration had an unusual opportunity for fresh diplomatic initiatives which, if well defined, were almost guaranteed to have a positive public reception and might well enjoy concrete policy success as well. Richard Nixon and Henry Kissinger proved to be a most effective combination for taking advantage of this situation. Concerning Vietnam, there was the image but not the reality of re-evaluation and a fresh approach to policy. On the other hand, regarding superpower and European affairs – in other words, the central policy concerns of the Atlantic Alliance – the new regime proved adept, imaginative and effective.

The new Nixon Administration represented a significant departure from what had gone before in several respects. First, the new government did not have the fixation with Vietnam at very senior levels that seemed to characterize the last three years of the Johnson Administration. In many ways, American war policy grew more ruthless, with much more extensive use of heavy bombing, including the secret strikes on Cambodia. Without doubt, Kissinger and others were very much engaged in the frustrating effort to extricate the United States from this unpopular, inconclusive war. But other important policy matters of consequence received attention as well. Notable among these were the rather subtle manipulations of the relationships between the United States and the two main Communist nations, the Soviet Union and China. If policy was not always structured along neat administrative lines, and if close allies in Europe and Asia were at times ignored, at least there was an effort to be comprehensive, to fit particular elements into a larger policy map of the world.

Second, the Nixon years witnessed the clear ascendancy of economic issues to a position which rivalled and in some ways surpassed military security concerns and those ideological worries which had been a defining characteristic of the Cold War years. To some extent, this represented a return to the more customary competition among relatively equal, or at least effectively distinct, economies which has usually been the state of affairs in the international system. The rigid equilibrium imposed on monetary values reflected, as did trade balances, the extraordinary – and unusual – dominance of the United States in international affairs for approximately two decades after the conclusion of the Second World War. By the end of the 1960s, this American hegemony in economic terms had undeniably come to an end. In the future, more nimble diplomacy would be required of a nation which could no longer rely automatically on the benefits provided by enormous economic power.

Finally, what have come to be viewed as the Nixon–Kissinger years saw the improvement to some extent of relations with selected European allies, including Britain, France and West Germany, though not necessarily because of the concrete foreign-policy efforts of Nixon and Kissinger. To be sure, ignoring U.S. allies to promote *détente* with China and the Soviet Union, and to secure the Salt treaties, had some negative consequences. Yet there was a new realism and restraint in Washington concerning what was expected in Atlantic Alliance relations, in part because of the misunderstandings of the early 1960s, and this helped improve the atmosphere. As so often in effective politics and diplomacy, good political judgement and fortunate timing were combined.

There were several factors which made for policy which was more consistent and inclusive, if not always more orderly, during the years of the Nixon Administration. First, the President was himself much more interested in the process and, especially, the substantive dimensions of foreign policy than had been the case with Johnson. He clearly prided himself on his experience in this field. During his tenure as Vice-President he had travelled extensively. He had maintained his international interests and contacts during the equally long period from 1961 to 1969 when he was out of office.

Second, in Henry Kissinger he had a deputy who was equally interested in the domination of the security process and had a comprehensive conception of the relations among the great powers to complement the ambitions of the President. In place of the increasingly decentralized, disorderly Johnson approach to policy, where attention was focused very heavily on Vietnam, and decisions were *ad hoc,* singular and characterized by discontinuity, Nixon and Kissinger placed a highly centralized system in operation. Attention was principally focused on great-power relations – the interplay among the Americans, the Soviets and the Chinese – and on the Vietnam War. Yet there was interest at the very top of the government in Atlantic Alliance relations as well. The allies were not granted priority, but arguably they had not really had it since Marshall Plan days. While extreme centralization did involve many problems, including lack of co-ordination – in particular, with the distrusted State Department – at least policy was informed by a general vision of where the country should go in international relations. Moreover, the fact that Europe was Kissinger's region of expertise, and Nixon had been Vice President when Europe was more clearly the centre of interest and involvement for U.S. foreign policy, facilitated such attention.[35]

Third, while there are fairly obvious shortcomings to an approach which centralizes power in the White House, the Nixon–Kissinger system was at least more coherent than the Johnson Administration's arrangements. In structure, there was apparently considerable dis-order from the start under Johnson, which only grew worse over time. In style, as noted, a preoccupation with Vietnam was replaced by a wider, more integrated view. While Johnson after assuming the presidency kept on Kennedy's senior foreign-policy officials, the chemistry and ties between the personalities involved changed greatly. One of the most perceptive analysts of the period described the situation as follows:

Bundy's foreign affairs operation went largely its own way . . . . To a considerable extent, the staff was turning into a shifting band of individuals and groups moving in mutual suspicion around the commanding, demanding figure of Lyndon Johnson.[36]

Nixon and Kissinger restored some order to foreign policy. Nixon began his term with a number of visits to senior European leaders, of whom the most interesting, for him as for others, was Charles de Gaulle. The two had a good rapport, again based on priority interest in foreign policy, and possibly an appreciation of the importance of personal tenacity in overcoming adversity in the long term. If de Gaulle remained basically hostile to the 'Anglo-Saxons', develop-ments in France and Europe helped to remove earlier tensions. De Gaulle retired from power in 1969 and his successor, Georges Pompidou, moved to improve relations with allies in very tangible terms, notably through agreement to the admission, at long last, of Britain to the European Community. This reflected the extraordinary growth of West Germany as a major force, economically and politi-cally, in the context of Europe, a development sufficiently worrisome to the French for them to view British entry as helping to provide a counterweight.[37]

The British also found the temperature in Washington more

pleasant, if only because the extreme frictions of the Johnson–Wilson relationship were a thing of the past. Nixon apparently had respect for Conservative Prime Minister Edward Heath (who succeeded Wilson following the general election of 1970), in part because the British leader had treated him well during the American's years of political exile. There were some similarities in the careers of the two men. Both had risen from comparatively modest origins, both were known for rather introverted, stiff styles in public and to some extent in private. If the relationship ultimately did not become a close one, at least they did work together with reasonable effectiveness. The fact that the long-term goal of British entry into the Common Market finally was achieved was satisfying to both sides. For the Americans, this had been a consistent foreign-policy goal for a number of years. On the British side, Heath had himself been centrally involved in the first initiative during the Macmillan government.

British policies continued to be influenced by economic realities. Though the Tories had raised the prospect during the election campaign of increasing defence spending, there was not in fact any major shift in real terms. Again, continuing economic weakness was more than enough to overcome lingering defence ambitions. By 1975, Britain was firmly focused in defence policies, as in economic policies, on Europe. Lingering commitments to various places around the globe did not alter this basic reality. Indeed, the Conservative government's inability to maintain, let alone expand, defence expenditures finally affirmed Britain's retreat from empire to Europe. The Conservative Party, in contrast to Labour, extols the imperial past, yet by the early 1970s even the most traditional imperialists were forced to reconcile themselves in practical policy terms to a continued reduction in defence spending and in international involvements outside Europe. Heath, who played a leading role in the early efforts to join the Common Market, found that his destiny included restoring Britain's primary focus on Europe in economic, political and military-security terms. When Labour replaced the Tories in power in 1974, first under Wilson, then under James Callaghan, the decision was taken to cut defence spending by a further £200 million over five years.[38]

A variety of factors, therefore, were encouraging more stable relations with European allies, including the Federal Republic of Germany. Willy Brandt's dramatic moves toward the East have already been described. A less troubled set of relations among Atlantic-area nations no doubt contributed to the success of accommodation with Moscow and key states of Eastern Europe. Kissinger states explicitly in his memoirs that the Nixon Administration was sympathetic to these efforts and assisted them, though not at the very start:

> Bonn would have faced a possible crisis with the East practically alone had it held to its earlier course. It was to Brandt's historic credit that he assumed for Germany the burdens and the anguish imposed by necessity.
> I cannot maintain that I came to this view immediately. But once I recognized the inevitable, I sought to channel it in a constructive direction by working closely with Brandt and his colleagues.[39]

Yet the success in stabilization with the East was a singular German accomplishment, further underlining the status of the nation as a major, and increasingly as the major, national force in Europe. Thus by the time Helmut Schmidt became federal chancellor in 1974, the political situation *vis-à-vis* the East had been stabilized as formal recognition of boundaries and territories indicated abandonment of old conflicts and old claims.

West Germany remained in many ways restricted on the internationl stage. The nation could not undertake to develop nuclear weapons. The Navy was strictly constrained, even though the Army was becoming the dominant one in conventional terms in Western Europe. Most important of all, of course, were the still-strong memories of the Second World War, and for that matter the First World War, with the attendant need to avoid any hint of militarism or aggressive revanchism. At the same time, the Federal Republic, freed from preoccupation over Berlin or national legitimacy, could become more active in wider European matters – and indeed in the wider Atlantic community, such as it was in the 1970s. Schmidt's West Germany thus became an increasingly prominent independent voice within the Alliance. As the 1970s wore on, he established a close rapport with French President Valéry Giscard d'Estaing. De Gaulle's effort to form *entente* through the 1963 treaty with Adenauer's Germany was thus confirmed.

These various improvements in bilateral relationships helped to overcome the divisive tensions created by economic and security developments. The early 1970s witnessed the start of two comprehensive multilateral negotiations designed to stabilize the environments in East and West Europe. The Mutual Balanced Force Reduction talks convened in Geneva in 1972. They resulted from an American initiative, first begun by President Johnson, to deflect energy from an initiative in the U.S. Congress – the Mansfield Amendment – for unilateral withdrawal of American troops from Western Europe. The M.B.F.R. talks, highly specific and technical in nature, focused on the range of conventional forces, including weapons and manpower levels and profiles. Not surprisingly, the talks soon became sunk in a morass of complex detail. Among other results, the Mansfield Amendment was undercut, which had been the principal goal of the effort by the White House.

During the same period, the Conference on Security and Co-operation in Europe (C.S.C.E.) began in Helsinki. This was a Soviet– Warsaw Pact initiative, designed at least in part to legitimize the division of Europe between East and West. The result was the treaty signed by President Ford, along with virtually all the other participating states' representatives, which in turn became a major issue within the Republican Party during Ronald Reagan's challenge to the President's renomination by his party in 1976. Critics in conservative quarters argued that the C.S.C.E. accord amounted to a Soviet trick to achieve legitimacy for their domination of Eastern Europe. The actual issues covered by the C.S.C.E. were comparatively abstract, dealing with human rights, military confidence-building and related measures. Rather formal recognition of the *de facto* border situation in Europe was the prime feature of the treaty that was seized upon by the far right in the United States.[40]

Both of these regional dialogues, of course, were overshadowed by the Strategic Arms Limitation Talks between the United States and the Soviet Union. The two 1972 Salt I treaties resulting from these negotiations, restricting offensive strategic land-based and sea-based nuclear launchers as well as defensive systems, arguably defined macroscopic nuclear-weapons relations between the two superpowers for the rest of the decade and were certainly a centrepiece of the Nixon–Kissinger policy of *détente*. By agreement at the start, European-theatre nuclear weapons were excluded from the talks. European allies similarly were excluded. As indicated, there was even a limit to the types of systems included in the negotiations. No doubt these restrictions were crucial to the success of the talks; however, tensions with and suspicions on the part of European allies were as a consequence inevitable. Given this situation, both M.B.F.R. and the C.S.C.E. were useful in Alliance political terms as exercises which helped to hold the partners together, providing a sense of involvement for the Europeans.

Similarly, the Nixon years witnessed considerable economic friction which complicated Alliance relations. Here again, the willingness and capacity of the American President to act decisively meant that problems were addressed even if Alliance relations did not improve as a result. The 1971 'Nixon shocks' involved the sudden, surprise announcement that the Americans were unilaterally disengaging from the letter and spirit of the Bretton Woods accords through imposition of a 10 per cent import surcharge and unhooking the value of the U.S. dollar from a fixed price of gold. There was an end to the convertibility of the dollar into gold for official claims. There was considerable anger overseas at the American action, but arguably Nixon and his advisers were simply facing, and forcing Europeans and Japanese to confront, the reality that the Bretton Woods trading and currency arrangements were already in crisis, inadequate to address or relieve the growing strains. U.S. trade imbalances were becoming unsustainable and the government could no longer honour actual and potential claims against the gold supply.[41]

Again, the problems of the economic sphere worked to highlight more general political developments for the remainder of the decade. In earlier years, U.S. economic dominance had created difficulties. Now, the balance of power among the major trading nations was much more equal. This change, which was among other things one of the goals of the Marshall Plan and other components of post-Second World War foreign policy, resulted in new problems. The oil shocks of 1973–4 further illustrated the capacity of economic change to drive wedges into the Alliance. Europeans may anyway have been less supportive of Israel than was Washington – certainly this was true of France – yet their much greater dependence on Arab oil for the working of industrial machines helped to widen the policy gap between the United States and its allies on Middle Eastern issues. The perceptions in Washington and major European capitals had changed greatly over the years since the Suez crisis of 1956, when the British and French sided with Israel in invading Egypt, and the United States forced all three nations to desist. As the United States became more firmly tied in alliance to Israel, problems grew with European allies, and oil dependency and Opec pricing-policies contributed very significantly to these tensions.

In summary, the international system of the 1970s, if less revolutionary than that of the 1960s, nevertheless contained many shifts and changes in bilateral and multilateral relations, and in the factors which were the focus of 'high politics' involving very senior foreign-policy officials. The Nixon Administration, ultimately discredited domestically, arguably addressed these changes in effective ways which protected fundamental national interests. Policy, if still too personalized and dominated by the President and his chief foreign-affairs deputy, nevertheless was much less disorderly than under Johnson and informed by a more consistent view of the world. At the same time, Alliance relations were made calmer by changes in European leadership and national policies.

5 Discontinuity, Uncertainty and Change: Atlanticism in Retreat

The Administration of President Jimmy Carter arguably represented a marked departure in style from what had gone before in domestic American politics, and – equally – in some important respects was very different from previous regimes in terms of foreign-policy themes and priorities. One should not carry this argument too far: the President, for all the emphasis on morality and modesty in power, was very much in tune with the mass-media and public-relations demands of modern American electoral politics. Only in retrospect, after the defeat in 1980 by Ronald Reagan, was the extraordinary accomplishment represented by Carter's electoral victory in 1976 overshadowed. Likewise, the Carter regime in different ways, including seeking arms accords with the Soviet Union and integrative overall themes to foreign policy, was very much in tune with the concerns of earlier administrations. The threat of nuclear war was a most central preoccupation, with the consequent strongly felt need to do something to control the strategic nuclear arsenals held by the superpowers. In this sense the interests of the President and his associates were consistent with those of U.S. foreign policy since the Eisenhower Administration.

None the less, the Carter Administration was in many ways – some simple and obvious but others more subtle – a change from the past. The President was the first true Southerner – from the deep South – to occupy the White House since before the Civil War. His victory was an enormous success for a man who started with not only the regional disadvantage but also very little national name recognition. His ability to employ the electoral primary system of the 1970s and the media potential to his advantage was distinctive and provided a model for future candidates. He was also arguably a good deal more conservative than the other Democrats who have achieved the White House in the last four decades. There were, therefore, various reasons for regarding President Carter and his Administration as unusual, and foreign-policy practice bore out this expectation.

There was a globalism to foreign-policy definition, at least early in the Carter Administration, which was distinctive and represented the strong conceptual influence of the President's Assistant for National Security Affairs, Zbigniew Brzezinski. The President was impressed, as he states in his memoirs, with Brzezinski's intellectual force and imagination, his capacity for integrative conceptualization and the lively manner in which he expressed himself. Carter was anxious to stress issues of third-world development and sought ways in which American foreign policy might be tied to these very different nations. He is probably the only U.S. president except for John Kennedy to have evinced a serious interest in African affairs, and his appointment of Andrew Young as Ambassador to the United Nations may be seen as one indication of the priority he gave to both Africa and the wider third world.

President Carter's interest in the third world clearly was closely tied, in his own mind and in the policies of his administration, with his strong emphasis on 'human rights' concerns and on the need to correct perceived abuses in that regard. Far from being a major departure, he saw this stress as being true to the best instincts of the American Republic:

> When I chose Andrew Young and Don McHenry to speak for us as Ambassadors to the United Nations, there was no doubt within the developing world that ours was an honest and sincere voice. We did not send a new message, but repeated for others to hear the same beliefs that had helped to form and shape our own country. Throughout Africa and the rest of the third world, there evolved a new confidence in what we had to say. [1]

The Carter Administration suffered from at least three different sorts of serious problem, each of which had an immediate and important bearing on Atlantic-area international relations. First, in organizational terms, the tension, which had become perennial, between the Secretary of State and Assistant for National Security Affairs went further, into a very open, intensely competitive conflict. Second, the general deterioration of the international economy, reflected in continuing inflation and the dominance of Opec, was a constant preoccupation which further represented the high political importance of economic matters. Economic challenges in turn led to the increased importance of the periodic summit meetings between the heads of government of North America, the major economies of Western Europe, and Japan. Third, arms and security issues presented serious problems for the Carter Administration and also revealed shortcomings in the President's decision style that soon came to plague Washington. President Carter has rightly been criticized for zig-zags and sudden shifts in policy, especially regarding arms and related matters in the context of Europe. In very specific terms, success in the negotiation of the Salt II treaty was hampered not only by the inability to secure U.S. Senate ratification of the understandings, but also by such missteps as the indecisiveness over deployment of the enhanced radiation warhead – the 'neutron bomb' – in Europe.

In many ways, the negative attitude taken, often out of hand, by so many who comment on the events of the Carter Administration, including foreign-policy matters, is excessive and undeserved. In retrospect, Carter seems almost refreshing intellectually compared with a Reagan Administration which has been quite reluctant to conceive or implement major policy departures in the realm of international concerns. As least Carter did work hard for a conceptual framework to guide definition and implementation of policy. Also, he did have solid foreign-policy successes as well as failures. The Camp David accords between Israel and Egypt were not entirely successful in that the dynamic of the peace process did not continue into an expanded, more inclusive regional peace involving the Arab states generally. Carter believes, and explicitly states, that he feels Prime Minister Begin went back on clear verbal understandings concerning Israeli West Bank settlements. Nevertheless, the Camp David treaty does stand as a major accomplishment in the continually vexing environment of the Middle East, and one which the successor administration in Washington has not been able to replicate.[2] Similarly, while Salt II was not ratified by the United States Senate, and President Carter complicated relations with that body by permitting himself to be quoted in the press to the effect that the treaty could be observed even if legislative endorsement were withheld, the agreement has been observed by both superpowers and has distinctive standing given the lack of progress since on arms-control accords.

In more practical policy terms, the Carter years were characterized by a constant, restless seeking of breakthroughs in other parts of the world, tied to human rights, nuclear non-proliferation and other urgent – if very complex – riddles, plus quite specific economic and security strains with European allies. Finally, the scene was overshadowed during Carter's last months by the plight of the American hostages held in Iran and the manner in which the President chose to address the situation over time. Human rights was used as a stick to beat governments closely allied with the United States in security terms, notably South Korea. A valiant effort was made to handle the problem of nuclear proliferation, and complex policy initiatives were devised; yet these seemed to have little effect, and, again, such moves as criticizing the Japanese for construction of a fast-breeder nuclear reactor at Tokai Mura and the West Germans for a nuclear sale to Brazil served to anger allies without having a measurable positive effect in terms of controlling the international proliferation problem.

These events bear on Atlantic Alliance relations and more strictly bilateral affairs between the United States and European allies, but they are not directly involved in Europe or the Nato area. Here, the Carter Administration witnessed considerable frustration. Perhaps the general tendency to view the Administration in negative terms is especially related to the downturn in Atlantic-area relations during the Carter years.

From the start, there were problems resulting from the competition between Secretary of State Vance and Security Assistant Brzezinski. Carter leaves no doubt about his respect for his National Security Assistant's intellectual qualities, while implying some reservations in the realm of practical policy judgement:

> To me, Zbigniew Brzezinski was interesting. He would probe constantly for new ways to accomplish a goal, sometimes wanting to pursue a path that might be ill-advised – but always thinking. . . . Next to members of my family, Zbig would be my favorite seatmate on a long-distance trip; we might argue, but I would never be bored.[3]

At the same time, and in contrast to Kissinger's tenure during Nixon's first term, the National Security Assistant did not establish a dominant role and the White House was not clearly the centre of power. Carter also has kind words in his memoirs for Cyrus Vance, and indeed apparently without guile notes that both Brzezinski and Vance had recommended the other for the job to which the man was appointed. 'In looking at my old notes, I find it interesting that Vance recommended Brzezinski for this job, and Zbig recommended Cy for Secretary of State. Both were good suggestions.'[4]

In effect, the stage was set, thanks in large part to the public visibility and assertiveness of Brzezinski, for a continuing conflict between the two officials. This was not resolved until Secretary Vance resigned over the effort to rescue the Iran hostages by force. For most of the Carter Administration, there was a constant contest between a security assistant inclined to think in theoretical and global terms, and a secretary of state who was traditional in background and experience, and closely tied to an Eastern Establishment which was so much associated with the Atlantic-based view of international affairs. Coherent policy suffered as a result.

Part of the problem no doubt was related to the President's rather poor relations with his counterparts in some of the allied Western nations. The later 1970s did witness the institutionalization of the periodic summits, begun under President Ford, of the seven major industrialized nations – the United States, Britain, Canada, France, West Germany, Italy and Japan. These provided an opportunity for co-ordination of policies and were seen as valuable enough to be worth holding fairly regularly. The standing of Japan as a major industrial nation, in many ways – though not all – part of the Western camp, was likewise recognized in an important way by these summits. In an age when the Bretton Woods procedures which had made international economic life orderly and rather predictable had gone by the board, these consultations, which included trade and monetary policies, have probably been invaluable. Yet during the Carter years they did also serve to highlight interpersonal frictions.

The outstanding example of poor chemistry between the American President and his counterparts were relations with the West German Chancellor, Helmut Schmidt. The leadership in Washington quickly came to mistrust the West German leader; Schmidt apparently considered Carter hopelessly parochial and unsophisticated. Certainly it is easy to see how a gulf would be present between the very secular European and the American Southerner who believed personal religion should be prominently featured in political dialogue. Carter writes in connection with the 1980 Venice economic summit, 'Shortly after arriving I had an unbelievable meeting with Helmut Schmidt . . . ranting and raving about a letter that I had written him, which was a well-advised message. He claimed that he was insulted. . . . Schmidt was quite emotional. When Zbig responded in a heated fashion, I tried to cool Zbig off. . . .'[5]

Schmidt for his part became over time more and more open in complaining about Carter. No doubt such incidents as the one over neutron-warhead deployment, where Schmidt took a political risk to support Washington only to have Carter suddenly change his mind, hurt the relationship. Never one to be accused of modesty, the Chancellor's rather casual approach to denigrating the leader of the most powerful member of Nato nevertheless raised eyebrows. A lengthy *New York Times Magazine* piece on Schmidt in the autumn of 1980 referred to his 'questionable judgment' in

> This continual talking down in private of Mr. Carter. It became a feature of Bonn life – every visitor to the Chancellor got a dose. . . . At two off-the-record seminars, attended by international policy makers, including the United States Ambassador to Bonn, Mr. Schmidt denigrated the American President and his capabilities.[6]

And so the relationship deteriorated during the remainder of Carter's tenure in office. In contrast to Eisenhower, who got along even with Charles de Gaulle; Kennedy, who was able to develop close rapport with Harold Macmillan; and Reagan, who seems to have established good communication with West German Chancellor Kohl (though the rocky elements in policy relations in the 1980s will also be examined below), Japanese Prime Minister Nakasone and British Prime Minister Thatcher, Carter did not seem to be able to build personal bridges to his counterparts among the major allies. Even the Nixon years, rife with complaints and suspicion about superpower dealings in secret, began to look benign in comparison with the troubled Carter period.

Interpersonal problems for the American President were compounded by the fact that a much stronger Franco-German relationship was emerging, fuelled by good personal rapport between President Giscard d'Estaing and Chancellor Schmidt. In policy terms, the closer understanding was helpful in tying the perennially uncertain French into the Alliance (in this connection it is instructive to remember Kennedy's remark about the wider value of the de Gaulle-Adenauer friendship treaty of 1963). However, in the circumstances of the later 1970s, the regular communication between Bonn and Paris seemed simply further to underline a real isolation on the part of Washington.

Author James Goldsborough has attempted to capture the tension of the times:

> Schmidt labeled President Carter 'unpredictable', and Giscard

spoke of keeping Europe out of Soviet–American 'bloc politics'. The Europeans criticized Washington's failure to consult before announcing the Olympic boycott and economic sanctions. The American Ambassador to Paris, Arthur Hartman, normally a discreet, behind-the-scenes diplomat, attacked the 'neutralist nonsense' he detected in French statements. American spokesmen condemned . . . spinelessness in the European stance.[7]

As noted, the summits provided a genuinely useful mechanism for interaction among the heads of the industrialized nations. These quickly became annual events. They were helpful in particular in handling economic conflicts, using specific *ad hoc* adjustments and arrangements in the midst of the general abandonment of the post-war Bretton Woods system of stable exchange rates and other regular institutionalized practices. President Carter, to his credit, was able to see the value of the summit meetings and consistently stressed their importance throughout his administration. They did reflect the increasing political significance of economic issues. By all accounts, he prepared for them rather assiduously and worked hard to make sure he had a maximum impact in policy terms. The interpersonal frictions which resulted, especially between Carter and Schmidt, should not be allowed to distract from the value of the exercises as vehicles of communication for the leaders.

ECONOMICS

The emphasis on allied summit meetings also underscored the point that economic concerns had by the second half of the 1970s achieved a position of paramount policy importance for a group of nations that had previously largely been preoccupied with military-security matters. Carter early in his tenure was confronted with another troubling episode in the continuing energy crisis, and that in turn contributed to the generally tension-filled atmosphere in his administration. The shortage of supply that had plagued the industrialized nations, and indeed the international system more generally, continued into his years in office.

There were very specific problems associated with the inability of the Administration to secure passage of an energy bill in the Congress. The President unfortunately had rather consistently poor relations with members of Congress, including the legislative leadership of his own party. Also, his emphasis overall on deregulation combined with a number of new regulations, while perhaps rational in an abstract sense, was guaranteed to antagonize a wide range of special-interest groups. Hence, the Administration's energy policies were soon stymied on Capitol Hill. The additional dramatic rise in Opec oil prices in 1979 did little to encourage domestic support for the President.

The continuing, apparently inexorable increases in oil and related energy prices were a preoccupation of the Administration as they were of policy-makers and analysts generally in Western nations. Thanks to the dramatic turnaround in the 1980s, with the consequent end of energy shortage and of escalation in energy prices that dominated the 1970s, it is rather easy now to minimize the enormous pressures the very different earlier situation generated. At the time, there was a strong sense in which the petroleum shortage seemed permanent. President Carter and his principal subordinates constantly searched for an interventionist, administrative solution to the problems. A *Wall Street Journal* article from early 1979 accurately sets the tone for the seemingly inescapable dilemmas:

As an incentive to increase domestic oil production, the Carter administration is considering a variety of ways to achieve a substantial increase in the price of petroleum.

The Energy Department said it is considering raising the price for newly discovered crude oil to world market levels, which are largely determined by the Organization for Petroleum Exporting Countries. This announcement follows an earlier disclosure that the department is looking into ways to increase the price of oil from most existing U.S. wells.

Together, the actions – neither of which requires legislation – could cost consumers billions of dollars.

Also, some officials privately say that the possibility of providing additional incentives to producers could be a handy bargaining chip to garner support for several legislative proposals, including a tax on crude oil, that the administration may seek this year. Such a tax would also mean a hefty rise in oil prices.

The department's latest proposal would establish a new category of oil under the government's complex pricing scheme. That category would be called 'newly discovered crude oil' and would receive the world market price at the time it is sold.[8]

ARMS

On the security side, the Administration enjoyed some successes, but here again the record was rather mixed and frustrating. Paul Warnke, the President's choice as head of the Arms Control and Disarmament Agency, was a man with very strong arms-control and security credentials. He had occupied senior positions in the Johnson Administration and was generally regarded as a central player in the arms-control fraternity. Carter's Secretary of Defense, Harold Brown, was also important as a player sympathetic to arms control, very much like his predecessor and mentor Robert McNamara. The President throughout his administration, in public statements and also more privately, maintained the strongest possible commitment to the goals of arms control

The Salt II treaty was negotiated with the Soviet Union, but as noted the Senate refused to ratify the agreement. Souring international events associated with the Soviet Union were one reason for this; however, the President once again complicated life for himself by the statement that the treaty could be observed by the executive even if Congress did not go along with ratification. The M.B.F.R. talks dragged on inconclusively.

While the Administration would in any case have had difficulty in selling Salt II to the Senate, Soviet moves elsewhere killed the treaty's prospects. Very specifically, the invasion of Afghanistan, and the U.S. reaction, ended whatever chances for passage had existed. Here again a case of sorts can be made for indecisiveness on the part of the White House. Earlier, the Soviets had taken control of the country through a brutal murder and a *coup d'état*. From their point of view, to send in troops in an overt occupation probably seemed a somewhat anticlimactic sequel rather than a fresh incursion; the American attitude, however, was quite different, and an administration which had acquiesced in the earlier move now reacted very strongly. A grain embargo was imposed on the Soviet Union, the United States decided to abstain from participation in the 1980 Olympic Games and asked other nations to do likewise.

The Salt II treaty, as negotiated, was extremely detailed. The number of variables contained was considerably greater than in the earlier Salt I exercise. The two Salt I treaties had focused on number of strategic-missile launchers. The Salt II treaty signed by Carter and Brezhnev in Vienna in mid-June 1979 contained a variety of ceilings on strategic systems, reflecting both an ambitious effort and a more complex strategic nuclear weapons environment.

Under Salt II, each side was limited to a total of 2250 ICBM and SLBM (submarine-launched ballistic missile) launchers and long-range bombers, which was a reduction from the ceiling of 2400 agreed upon at the Vladivostok meeting in 1974 between Brezhnev and President Ford. There were a series of further sub-limits in the agreement: 1320 on all types of mirved launchers (i.e. those capable of handling *m*ultiple *i*ndependently *t*argetable *r*e-entry *v*ehicles), 1200 for mirved SLBM and ICBM launchers, and 820 for mirved ICBMs alone. There was also a restriction on missile size, with both sides prohibited from developing new ICBMs larger than the Soviets' giant SS-19. The Soviets specifically agreed not to add to the 308 very large ICBM launchers they already had in place.

The Administration in the first months in office had faced a serious reversal when two proposals for reductions, one involving very deep cuts, had been rejected publicly and out of hand by the Soviets, a surprise to the White House and particularly embarrassing for the Secretary of State. Months passed before the negotiations were brought back on track. The final achievement of the Salt II treaty with the Soviets must have provided great satisfaction to those involved, given the tremendous effort expended, the earlier frustration and the President's continuing commitment to arms control as a policy priority. While the U.S. Senate did not provide the ultimate ratification of the treaty, both superpowers generally have abided by the understandings. In consequence, attention was focused for a time, before the strategic departures of the Reagan Administration, on the theatre nuclear weapons dimension, i.e., those of shorter ranges than systems covered in Salt. This was to be the next arena for regulation of the arms race, assuming that strategic understandings on intercontinental systems remained in place.

Arguably, the effort to keep European allies informed about security developments was more serious and conscientious during the Carter Administration than under Nixon and Kissinger. At the same time, however, Europeans were as usual afraid that somehow their own security interests would be sacrificed by the Americans. Also, the approach that Carter took to specific issues and crises inevitably complicated life with Europe. The gas-pipeline controversy, the about-face on the enhanced-radiation warhead, and the reaction to the invasion of Afghanistan, including the American-led boycotts of the Olympic Games and trade with the Soviet Union, all complicated life with the Europeans. There was a fairly constant refrain that the Americans were neglecting European affairs in striving to reach accommodation with the Soviet Union.

This all helps to explain the so-called 'two-track' decision taken by Nato members in 1979. This decision reflected European pressures on the United States, felt so often in the past, to demonstrate unmistakable commitment to European security. In this case, a particular effort was also made to couple the understanding to deploy 572 new missiles with attempts at further arms negotiations with the Soviet Union.

This was not the first time that Washington had placed missiles on the ground in Europe as a means of demonstrating, indeed symbolizing in basic terms, the U.S. security guarantee and the fact that nuclear weapons were a fundamental part of the American commitment to Europe. During the Eisenhower Administration, Jupiter and Thor missiles had been positioned on European soil for essentially the same reasons. These systems in Europe were reduced during the Kennedy Administration precisely because sea-based weapons were recognized to be more secure in purely military terms. In the 1979 decision, agreement was reached that the Alliance would begin to deploy 464 new cruise and 108 Pershing II missiles to counter the threat posed by the continuing build-up of Soviet mirved SS-20 mobile missiles. The Nato allies did stress at the time that equal weight would be given to the effort to reach negotiated arms agreements with the Soviets. The decision to deploy the new missiles is understandable in the context of the insecurity felt by Europeans and fresh worries about Soviet designs and ambitions, not only in Europe but elsewhere in the world.

The particular missiles selected could be seen as especially worrisome for Moscow. This was in line with Nato goals of showing the Soviets that the decision was meaningful rather than ceremonial; none the less, for this very reason the other side was given maximum incentive to try to undermine the initiative. The cruise missile is an exceptionally sophisticated weapon, more like a pilotless aircraft than a ballistic missile. The cruise can follow a predetermined course that does not have to be a straight line, and can meander, even go in the reverse direction, in order to throw off surveillance. While susceptible to anti-aircraft fire and for that matter other aircraft, the cruise can hug terrain features at low altitude in order to escape radar detection. The weapon is air-breathing, which further adds to flexibility and manoeuvrability. To some extent, in terms of basic technology, the cruise is similar to the V-1 rocket, or 'buzz bomb', used by the Germans during the Second World War. While the Soviets have reportedly struggled with this technology since the end of the 1950s, they have apparently had only limited success with their efforts. This weapon, reminiscent of the last-ditch technological efforts of the hated Germans, symbolic of the power and finesse of American technology, could not be better designed to play on Soviet insecurities.

Likewise, the Pershing II missile is guaranteed to be worrisome to the Soviets. While the exact flight time of the missile is classified, a reasonable estimate is in the neighbourhood of ten minutes. Moreover, unlike the Pershing I, the new version has the capacity to strike Soviet territory, thanks to its decidedly longer range. Hence, the incentive pre-emptively to destroy Pershing II bases first in the event of crisis or limited conflict is very great. Arguably, deployment of the missiles raises the tension level on both sides of the dividing-line between the Eastern and Western blocs in Europe. The characteristics of the Pershings in particular led to second thoughts on the part of the Europeans.

The Nato partners gave plenty of warning of the new deployment. The Nato Nuclear Planning Group gathered in Florida on 24 and 25 April 1979, and rather quickly reached accord in formal terms that the Alliance required new deployments of comparatively long-range missiles to counter the Soviets, specifically the SS-20 weapons system. Nato Secretary General Joseph Luns and U.S. Defense Secretary Harold Brown joined in a final statement to the press at the end of the meeting that the modernization of Soviet forces had been a matter of primary concern. According to the communiqué issued at the end of the meeting,

> In their consideration of Nato's requirements, as part of the Long-Term Defense Program, to modernize theater nuclear forces, the Ministers reaffirmed that Nato could not rely on conventional forces alone for credible deterrence in Europe; and that, without increasing dependence on nuclear weapons or prejudicing long-term defense improvements in conventional forces, it would be necessary to maintain and modernize theater nuclear forces.
>
> As a key element in this and taking into account developments in Soviet capabilities, the Ministers continued their consideration of modernization of the longer range theater-based element in support of the Alliance's strategy of forward defense and flexible response,

for preserving a credible capability in that field. No decisions were taken at this stage. The Ministers emphasized that consideration of a modernization effort would need to take full account of arms control possibilities and they noted with approval that these are being studied in further depth by a special group recently set up in NATO for this purpose . . . .[9]

Over time, there were clear and growing anxieties on the part of various political quarters in Europe about the deployment of these particular weapons. Parties on the left, especially when out of government, predictably came out against them. Intense debates took place in the Labour Party in Britain, the Social Democratic Party in West Germany and other parties in Europe, notably in the Low Countries. What had begun as an American effort to respond to European pressures ended with American insistence that the missiles originally agreed to be deployed.

To the credit of the Carter Administration, once the decision had been made in this case there was continuity over time, in some contrast to the handling of the neutron-warhead decision. The long lead time involved in the deployment, and the extensive publicity accompanying the decision, also permitted the build-up of substantial opposition pressures from the political left in Europe. Again, the Carter Administration's reputation for ineffectiveness added to the difficulties. For some Europeans, and not just those on the left, the uncertainties involved in the Salt II Treaty became tangled with the deployment decision. The *New York Times* reported in October 1979 that,

> Representatives of parliaments in the Atlantic alliance have begun to deliver sharp warnings that failure of the Soviet-American arms treaty could lead to refusal by the allies to accept new United States nuclear weapons.
>
> The need for Senate approval of the treaty before further moves to strengthen the atomic arsenal in Europe was put implictly in a report titled 'Alliance Political Developments' prepared for approval by the North Atlantic Assembly to be held in Ottawa later this month. [10]

Likewise, Chancellor Schmidt of Germany used opportunities created by the image of American uncertainty to assert his own nation's independence and indirectly criticize his rival. In March 1980, for example, there were reports that West Germany was reminding other European nations that the American President had done an about-face on the neutron warhead and might do the same in connection with his threat of an Olympic Games boycott if the Soviets did not withdraw from Afghanistan by 20 February. [11]

The Soviets almost immediately sought to take advantage of the possibilities the two-track decision represented for encouraging possible divisions within the Alliance. Any other reaction would in fact have been surprising, given the combination of difference of view in Europe and Soviet anxieties. In early October, Soviet President Brezhnev declared during a speech in East Berlin commemorating the thirtieth anniversary of the establishment of the German Democratic Republic that up to 20,000 troops and 1000 tanks would be removed from East Germany during the following twelve months. He declared ominously that 'The proponents of the arms race use any, and one can even say nonexistent, invented, pretexts to heat up the atmosphere and whip up military preparations.'

The Carter Administration responded quickly; although the two-track decision was not taken formally until December, the Brezhnev statement was viewed as an effort to sidetrack a more modest earlier plan to deploy a smaller number of missiles. The *New York Times* reported,

> Carter Administration officials said today that Leonid I. Brezhnev's speech in East Berlin seemed part of a concerted Soviet effort to persuade West European countries not to go along with allied plans to deploy nearly 600 new nuclear-armed missiles in Europe.

The article quoted Brezhnev and went on to state that the Administration accepted none of the Soviet leader's criticism of the plans to deploy new missiles, which were expected to be approved at the December Nato meetings. Later, when deployment of the missiles had been formally approved by the Nato allies, the Soviets responded very quickly, declaring that the decision was the result of 'crude pressure' by the United States and 'dangerous to the cause of peace and to international detente'. [12]

The divisions the two-track decision engendered in West European political parties of the left were equally apparent. In particular, difficulties quickly surfaced in the Social Democratic Party of West Germany:

> Egon Bahr, the secretary-general of the West German Social

Democratic Party, is used to being the center of controversy and he is so once again.

His opposition to the stationing of medium-range nuclear weapons in West Germany that could reach the Soviet Union has led to a major disagreement with Chancellor Helmut Schmidt.[13]

As usual, the French pursued an independent course, making clear that there was commitment to the Alliance in the event of war while also indicating that the national nuclear force would remain separate prior to the ultimate catastrophe. The specific national policy remained that, until European unity became a practical political fact, France would guard the independence of national military forces. In October 1979, for example, Olivier Stirn, Deputy Foreign Minister, declared in the National Assembly that

> France, which is not a member of the Nato integrated military organization, is not party to the studies currently being made by these allies on modernizing theater weapons. The French government has let it be known publicly that it will not take part in the SALT III negotiations[14]

Again, the very good personal rapport between French President Giscard d'Estaing and West German Chancellor Schmidt, and the lack of rapport between either leader and President Carter, contributed to French independence through development of the Franco-German *entente*.

Almost immediately, the missile initiative posed special political problems for the West German government. Never mind that the Schmidt regime had been insistent initially on receiving the missiles, only later to back-pedal in the face of pressure from the left in the Social Democratic Party. Now there were comparatively strong pressures beyond the left wing of the party urging at least second thoughts on the agreement to accept the missiles. The rub for the West Germans came in the fact that all the Pershing II missiles would be on their soil. Initially the Germans had insisted that at least one other country on the continent (i.e. besides Britain) should agree to take some of the 572 new missiles. The Belgians and the Italians agreed to accept cruise missiles, so that initial problem was solved. However, the Pershings remained concentrated on West German soil, and therefore presumably served to single out West Germany from the rest of continental Europe as a prime target.

The resulting tensions were clear in news reports in connection with Chancellor Schmidt's scheduled visit to Moscow in the middle of 1980. Schmidt took advantage of the opportunity provided by the agreement to deploy the new missiles in Europe to try to undertake some creative diplomacy with the Soviet side. In specific terms, he tried to take the lead with the Soviet Union in an effort to slow down, delay or stop deployment of their missiles. To some extent, he was able to take advantage of a European perception that leaders there were more willing to engage in serious arms-control negotiations with the Soviets for significant mutual reductions of nuclear forces. By contrast, Washington, according to this argument, was preoccupied with the deployment of new forces and insufficiently sensitive to the possibilities that might exist for genuine East–West arms negotiations and understandings on these matters.

IRAN

Overshadowing all else, however, during the last year of the Administration was the hostage crisis in Iran. Carter, in his usual detailed, dispassionate manner, is explicit in his memoirs concerning the degree to which the developing Iranian crisis loomed over and threatened the foreign-policy goals of his administration:

> On January 4, 1979, I went to Guadeloupe to meet with the leaders of France, Great Britain, and Germany, but I had to spend a great deal of my time working on the Iranian crisis. Secretary of State Vance stayed in Washington with the Vice President to monitor the situation in Tehran. My instructions had been to do everything possible to strengthen the Shah, but during these days I became increasingly troubled by the attitude of Ambassador Sullivan, who seemed obsessed with the need for the Shah to abdicate without further delay . . . .

In this foreign-policy dilemma as in others, not just in the Carter Administration, a president was frustrated by his sense that the State Department was not fully loyal in carrying out his directives. Carter is especially critical of the U.S. ambassador to Iran, William Sullivan, but is also more generally negative about the State Department's role in the situation:

I became even more disturbed at the apparent reluctance of the State Department to carry out my directives fully and with enthusiasm. Its proper role was to advise me freely when a decision was being made, but then to carry it out and give me complete support once I had issued a directive. Cy sent one of his deputies to Iran to straighten out Sullivan or remove him, and I asked the Iranian desk officers and a few others to come to the White House.[15]

Ultimately, of course, the Iranian crisis helped to oust Carter from the presidency. While speculation can be endless, and pointless, there is comparatively little doubt that his prospects against Ronald Reagan in the 1980 presidential campaign would have been considerably enhanced had the hostages been freed, either through negotiation or a successful rather than disastrous military rescue mission. While criticism is easy after the event and from a removed position, the point remains that Carter seemed to develop a near-fixation on the Iran crisis during the last year of his presidency. Arguably, apart from damaging himself politically, he also played into the hands of the radical, fundamentalist Iran regime through his constant attention to the problem, which only served to underscore American frustration.

Perhaps an instructive comparison is the Pueblo crisis which plagued President Johnson during his final months in office. In that case, the North Koreans seized an American ship and held the crew hostage, accompanying their action with various demands. Although Johnson was hardly a restrained or unassuming president, he did exercise remarkable forbearance in this particular case. Through self-discipline, the Administration was able to get the case out of the headlines and off the front pages. Some months later, the North Koreans released the crew, abused but alive. The Ayatollah Khomeini in Iran probably would not have permitted quite that degree of media neglect, but the fact remains that Carter's constant emphasis on the crisis did not hasten release of the hostages and indeed placed his entire foreign policy in a captive position. Certainly, events in the Gulf overall in different ways discouraged co-operation among the Atlantic area allies.

Was the Carter Administration the failure so many in the press and elsewhere declared at the time and have argued since? Certainly not. The Camp David accords stand as a major diplomatic achievement, largely though not entirely respected by those who signed them. The Salt II treaty, though not formally ratified, has generally been respected by the United States and the Soviet Union. More broadly, the President's sincere emphasis on human-rights concerns could not have seriously damaged Alliance relations, which were otherwise strong, and did serve to draw attention to basic ethical considerations.

Yet the Carter Administration's handling of Alliance relations does compare unfavourably with that of the Nixon–Kissinger regime. Above all, the former leaders seemed to implement policies that were consistent and informed by a practical, if at times too cynical, view of the world. By contrast, the Carter foreign policy was informed by a lofty, theoretical perspective which seemed to translate unfortunately into inconsistent and sometimes directly competing policies. Nixon and Kissinger followed a consistent triangular diplomacy that involved playing the Soviets and Chinese off against one another, while at the same time keeping their allies in Europe and Japan at some distance. Carter oscillated between the global visions of Brzezinski, whose attraction lay in his attempts to develop fresh, imaginative conceptions of the international system, and the traditional Atlanticism of Vance, who offered security, reliability and the conventional view.

At heart the problem was, of course, that the President appeared to be especially indecisive – and, perhaps worse, was seen publicly to be so afflicted – in his inability to embrace fully either competing foreign-policy perspective. Others could play the gamesman who has competing subordinates but still appears to be in charge (Kennedy) or the statesman who moves above the daily fray (Eisenhower and perhaps Reagan), but Carter more than any other post-war president seemed trapped in a swamp of his own creation, immersed in detail, publicly changing his mind on important issues. The zig-zagging on security matters, for example, was underscored by the destructive competition between Vance and Brzezinski.

Carter himself was aware of the problem. While at some points he has seemed to acknowledge the fundamental flaws in his foreign-policy structure, he remains basically defensive and appears to ascribe the problems more to the press and the personality contrasts between his two principal deputies:

> Zbig is a little too competitive and incisive. Cy is too easy on his subordinates. And the news media constantly aggravate the inevitable differences and competition between the two groups. I hardly know the desk officers and others in State, but work very closely with N.S.C. people. When we have consulted closely, like in the

Mideast area, at Camp David, and otherwise, we've never had any problems between the groups.[16]

In the Atlantic area, as with the domestic electorate, the Carter years brought a desire for stronger, more decisive American foreign-policy leadership. Reagan, a conservative Republican, in tune with perceptions that greater efforts in defence and greater consistency in foreign policy were needed, swept to a decisive electoral victory in the United States with no particular foreign-policy agenda. Though his style and background were hardly likely to be in tune with even conservative Europeans, so great was the alienation from the Carter Administration that the new Republican regime had an automatic initial advantage in dealing with Alliance matters.

ATLANTIC AND PACIFIC

The successors to the Carter Administration would be faced with one very large-scale development with clear implications for Atlantic-area relations as traditionally conceived: the emergence of the Pacific basin as the principal realm of U.S. trade involvement. In 1981, Asia sur-passed Europe by a slight margin in total annual volume of trade with the United States. In the years since, this margin has grown steadily wider. Greater U.S. trade involvement has led naturally to concern that security priorities should follow suit. Despite the fact that Ameri-cans are not engaged in direct combat in Asia, as they were during the Korean and Vietnam wars, worry has grown in Europe that Washing-ton is increasingly focusing primary attention there.

Some actions taken by the Carter Administration towards the end of its life arguably increased this tendency. For instance, in spring 1980 the President agreed to a new overall strategic conception that no longer committed Washington to send Pacific-based forces to Europe in the event of a Soviet invasion. While the true nature of the change remained ambiguous, apparently Washington was making the point that the traditional 'swing strategy', in which protection of Nato ter-ritory was paramount, was being abandoned in favour of a more flexible approach. Among other things, the argument ran, this recog-nized the importance of the Persian Gulf as a source of vital oil supplies and permitted the Americans to keep their options more open in case of crisis. The *New York Times* quoted a 'senior Pentagon official':

> We now have more flexibility to determine if and when this would be necessary [i.e. to commit U.S. forces to Europe]. We may have to keep our forces in the Pacific, move them into the Indian Ocean or send them to Western Europe. It will depend on the circumstances.[17]

As with so much in the Carter approach to foreign policy, no particular concrete policy gains were to be had from declarations which nevertheless complicated relations with allies. The quest for pristine clarity was grating on the nerves of friendly nations. A more relaxed approach, which accepted ambiguity as unavoidable, at times even desirable, would have been better. This, however, ran counter to the basic thrust of foreign policy during the Carter years. Consequently, the natural advantage of a new administration was heightened for President Reagan and his colleagues. Fairly or unfairly – and the argument here is that both terms are apt – the Carter Administration had been accused generally of ineffectiveness and indecisiveness in foreign policy. Hence, the domestic American political situation played to Reagan's demonstrated strengths: not necessarily the reality of decisiveness, but the image of a strong, forceful leader, in the traditional American patriotic mould. The test of course was whether image could be made to match reality in a manner which also allowed sensible foreign policy toward Atlantic-area allies.

THE REAGAN ADMINISTRATION

The Reagan Administration represents both the stability of traditional American conservatism and the more strident, populist, unpredictable rightist ideology which has been in the post-war period a changing but ever-present force in American political life. If President Reagan draws some of his themes, and much of his most committed support, from the extreme right, he has also been able to draw on earlier, more broadly appealing concepts which have traditionally defined the Republican Party. At times, the style and substance are both rather reminiscent of the years of Dwight Eisenhower and Robert Taft, the late 1940s and the 1950s, in the life of the party and the nation. Stability, continuity and restraint, which are among the virtues appreciated by those earlier statesmen, are combined with the alarmist tone and pugnacious rhetoric of the contemporary extreme conservatives. In part, Reagan's political genius is to combine both dimensions in his style in a credible way. That style has important implications for public policy in general, including foreign-policy considerations.

The Reagan Administration's congruence with more traditional American conservatism can be seen in different ways, including the lack of dramatic departures in diplomatic affairs. In the 1952 presidential campaign, much was made of the prospects of 'liberation' of East European areas controlled by the Soviet Union. Many believe continuing emphasis on this theme in American radio propaganda gave some impetus to the Hungarian revolt of 1956. In the event, of course, the Eisenhower Administration's belligerent anti-Communist rhetoric, emanating notably from Secretary of State Dulles, was combined with great restraint in consideration of the actual use of force. If anything, the successor Kennedy Administration was more adventurous in a willingness directly to employ the U.S. military overseas. The Reagan Administration, for all its aggressive rhetoric, has so far been rather reluctant to send and use ground forces abroad, with the singularly disastrous exception of the Middle East, and the very controlled circumstances of Grenada.

The more adventurous, populist side of the conservative movement can probably be seen most significantly in the Strategic Defense Initiative (S.D.I.) of the Administration, a policy departure which has had an especially important impact on Euro-American relations. The significant military build-up undertaken by Reagan officials, the efforts to bolster the government of El Salvador and overthrow that of Nicaragua, and the apparent lack of interest in serious arms-control negotiations and accords with the rival superpower are in line with this other dimension of conservatism. Each, beyond the special case of the S.D.I., has a bearing on Atlantic Alliance relations.

Ronald Reagan throughout the 1980 presidential campaign stressed themes of strength and decisiveness, arguing that the Carter Administration had been characterized by neither, and the release at last of the American hostages held in Iran just as the inaugural ceremonies in Washington were getting under way lent a touch of drama to the proceedings while appearing to symbolize that the new style in Washington was able to get results. Whether or not the President in fact would be a strong leader in terms of directly acting in crises – comparable, for example, to Eisenhower – is still debatable. The nation has been spared, at least so far, another Indochina or Suez; use of force in Grenada and Libya has been on a lesser order of magnitude. What is undeniable is that the image of strength has helped the President in domestic politics and arguably has been an asset for American foreign policy as well.

In organizational terms, the Reagan Administration tried from the start to set up a contrast with the internal competition of the Carter years in foreign policy. This was done with only partial success. Richard Allen, the new president's National Security Adviser, was in the news primarily to advertise his self-effacing approach to the job, an approach different from that taken by Brzezinski and others. For structural reasons the position was also considerably less senior than it had been before – Allen did not have regular access to the President in the same way as his predecessors had. He had to go through the so-called White House 'troika' of aides James Baker, Edwin Meese and Michael Deaver.

Allen also had a cerebral rather than administrative conception of the position. He was quoted to this effect:

> The important thing to me is the shape of policy in two or three years. That's the ultimate test. And anonymity helps in getting the job done. . . .
> I've told my colleagues, 'If you're looking for action in terms of day-to-day operations, sending out cables and circulating memos, this is not the place for you – you should be out in the operating agencies. But if you are interested in seeing the policy-making machinery mesh in a coherent and intelligent fashion and you want to be at the crossroads of policy making and you're interested in longer-term policy initiatives, then this is the place for you'.[18]

Ultimately, this approach proved to be unsatisfactory for the President and others in the Administration. The personal staffing needs of the Chief Executive, which have consistently tended to emphasize different kinds of administration, were not well handled under Allen and he was replaced. His successors, William Clark, Robert McFarlane and John Poindexter, have been precisely the sort of administrators that a succession of presidents have felt they needed and demanded.

The change of national security adviser was paralleled by a change of secretary of state. From the beginning, Alexander Haig made clear that he would be a dominant figure in the formulation and implementation of foreign policy. Almost immediately, there were tensions with others in the Administration, including in particular the dominant

White House aides Baker, Deaver and Meese. Right after the inauguration of President Reagan, Haig presented a detailed memorandum which would have given him extraordinary authority over the conduct of the nation's international affairs. In March 1981, *Time* magazine featured Haig in a cover story entitled 'The "Vicar" Takes Charge', which began as follows:

> The meeting in the Oval Office was private, but after it ended White House aides invited photographers to snap pictures of Ronald Reagan and his Secretary of State. Explained one staffer: 'We need to show that the Secretary has access to Reagan.' Replied another: 'You've got it wrong. We need to show that the President has access to Al Haig.'[19]

From the very start, therefore, there was serious tension between a secretary of state who sought to be a very dominant, very visible figure, and a president who stressed team play and largely succeeded in gathering around him a senior group of aides who accepted that point of view. In the latter part of 1982, after apparently several threats by Haig to quit, the President finally accepted his resignation and George Shultz, a much more low-key, collegial and undramatic individual assumed the post.

Despite the changes in the personalities at the top there were positive developments for West European governments during the tenures of both Haig and Shultz. One of Haig's first and most positive steps was to downplay the pressure on the Europeans, which had been relentless for months, to live up to the agreement to increase defence spending by 3 per cent annually in real terms (i.e. after inflation). He knew considerably more than others at senior levels of the Administration about the viewpoints of the Europeans and was aware, for example, that they had generally been more consistent than the United States in defence spending. While the United States had reduced defence spending with the waning of the Vietnam War, only to decide toward the end of the 1970s again to expand that sector of the budget, the Europeans had been more even in their spending-patterns over time. With the exception of the British (who have consistently spent a larger share of gross national product on defence), they had also generally retained military conscription. Thus Haig, if he confronted a series of 'turf battles' and interpersonal disputes during his brief tenure as Secretary, was very helpful in bridging the perception gap between the Europeans and the Americans.

The Pipeline and Economic Relations

Likewise, George Shultz was able to mitigate an important dispute between the Americans and the Europeans, in this case over the gas pipeline. The tensions arose from an agreement among the French, Italian, West German and Soviet governments for the transmission of natural gas. The Soviets made a commitment to transport 40,000 million cubic meters of natural gas, above the 23,500 million already being shipped, in return for loans and equipment to assist in the construction of a 3500-mile-long pipeline from Western Siberia to the border of Czechoslovakia. Initial discussions on the deal took place in 1978, and the final agreements were reached at the end of 1981.

The negative American reaction to the understandings was motivated apparently by a combination of ideological hostility and practical concern about dependence on Soviet sources for a vital fuel. One analyst has described the situation as follows:

> The first immediate consequence of the American embargo of December 1981 was to block the General Electric Company in the United States and its European licensees from exporting key components for the gas turbine compressors the Soviets had ordered for the East–West pipeline. This forced the Soviets to reconsider their plans . . . since only one of GE's European licensees was able to produce the needed components. . . .[20]

In June 1982, the US government increased the pressure by restricting the transfer of technology and equipment to European subsidiaries of American firms. These moves forced the Soviets to turn more to their own resources, and created difficulties with European allies, but did not sidetrack the pipeline deal. While intense and pressured, the crisis atmosphere did not last that long; in November the Americans abandoned these sanction efforts.

More generally, economic relations during the Reagan Administration have been difficult but not in crisis. This has not been a direct result of assertive economic initiatives from Washington. There has been resentment of the high interest rates resulting from U.S. fiscal policies, and of the related attraction of investment capital from Europe to the American markets. Overall, however, relations have certainly been no worse than during the Carter years. Unemployment has remained high and growth sluggish in most industrialized nations, but the tensions resulting directly from the high inflation of the 1970s have been dissipated. Moreover, the uncertainty and change in the trade and monetary systems since Bretton Woods was abandoned in 1971 may simply have become more tolerable over time. Sudden shocks are still unwelcome, but we have become more used to an environment which is no longer new.

Yet the international economic system remains far removed from the stable, in retrospect sunny, relations before the Nixon shocks of 1971. Previously the United States had held *de facto* economic sway and had been able to underwrite stability through the governing-mechanisms for trade and monetary policy established at the conclusion of the Second World War. In spring 1981, early in the Reagan administration, the *Wall Street Journal* published a perceptive piece relating economic issues to security concerns in the context of Nato. Owing to the points made, it is worth quoting at some length:

> BRUSSELS – In a sprawl of low buildings on the outskirts of town are the headquarters of the North Atlantic Treaty Organization. It is the administrative center of the Western defense alliance, a sort of transatlantic Pentagon.
>
> These days, however, many of the people inside are sounding more as though they worked in a transatlantic Treasury. They are talking of inflation and unemployment, interest rates and oil prices, social security and welfare, trade and aid, and the problems of spurring economic growth.
>
> Their talk is anything but idle. Many analysts in Europe and the U.S. think that such pocketbook issues may well be among the most important – and most divisive – problems facing the Nato alliance over the next decade.
>
> 'Economic policy is vital, and it relates directly to our security policy', says a senior economist at Nato. 'A successful economic policy may have to be the very basis of a resurgent defense policy.'
>
> That possibility matters to the United States as it tries to persuade the Nato allies to increase their defense spending at a time when their sluggish economies are forcing many of them to slash popular social programs. . . .[21]

The Reagan Administration, while not attempting a wholesale dismantling of the modern welfare system (and especially sensitive on the issue of social security), is none the less very strongly committed to defence-spending increases and limiting or cutting back other sectors of the federal budget. Consequently, on the economic front, there is an inherent tension between what the Americans are trying to achieve and what the Europeans insist upon as their own priorities. In these terms, a conservative Republican administration in Washington, pressing allies to spend more on defence, is bound to generate frictions with West Europeans.

Defence Issues

There was a significant shift from the Carter to the Reagan Administration in military and related security affairs. To be sure, the second half of Carter's presidential term had been characterized by emphasis on doing more in military affairs, with specific reference to the 3 per cent understanding for increased defence spending. However, under Reagan the emphasis on military efforts has been vastly greater, and senior civilian decision-makers have been far more sympathetic to the military. The Reagan Administration has been committed from the very beginning to a very significant increase in military spending, to a total of $1600 million more over five years. This represents a genuinely fundamental shift in priorities compared with the Carter years. Obviously there are important implications for Nato in a greatly expanded U.S. military effort.

At the same time, for at least two major reasons the Reagan defence emphasis has not had the impact on Nato affairs that might otherwise have been expected. First, there have generally been conservative governments in power in Europe. The Thatcher government in Britain has been very much on the same wavelength as the conservative American Administration. In West Germany, while Schmidt's tensions with Carter had been legendary, there seemed to be early rapport with Reagan. Early in 1981, Chancellor Schmidt and French President Giscard d'Estaing met for the thirty-seventh Franco-German summit meeting. They stressed afterwards that they were anxious to 'work in harmony and trust with the new American administration'. They also emphasized in effect their joint belief in a strong, assertive European diplomatic role.[22] Four days after talks with the American President, the West German Chancellor won overwhelming parliamentary support for the Nato weapons modernization programme. Only six members of the *Bundestag* voted against this initiative. The Kohl government has been particularly well disposed to American policies; Chancellor Kohl's relationship with the American President survived even the controversial Bitburg cemetery visit in the late spring of 1985.

Second, the Reagan build-up has not been accompanied by any

major change in strategic doctrine in so far as Nato is directly concerned. Indeed, except for some initial attention to salary increases, the
American defence increase has been concentrated primarily on major
weapons systems, expansion of which has been supported virtually
across the board, with no serious effort to differentiate among them.
There has been no conceptual shift comparable to the 'New Look'
Eisenhower years, with their stress on nuclear weapons, or the Kennedy years, with their attention to counter-guerrilla and conventional
military capabilities.

Rather, the Reagan Administration has spent a great deal more on
defence without any particular doctrine underlying the effort. Consequently, the Europeans have not had to respond to specific American pressures to do more in the conventional or, for that matter, other
military fields. Generally in the past, new American efforts have been
accompanied by pressures on the Europeans to do more also; this
time, the Americans are spending more without any particular sus-
tained emphasis on the Europeans' doing more in a concrete sense.
Hence tension has been present but manageable.

This is related to one of the most serious, and perhaps ultimately
among the most telling, criticisms of the Reagan Administration. With
the expansion of the defence budget have come charges of waste and
mismanagement in the allocation of funds. Such complaints are always
present, but have been very strong during the Reagan years and have
been combined with allegations that Secretary of Defense Caspar
Weinberger has not been a strong manager of the Pentagon over time.
The Secretary's unwillingness to demonstrate flexibility in dealing with
a Congress growing less enthusiastic about defence since 1981 has
further complicated the Administration's political situation.

There have also been specific complaints that more funds are not
more useful unless combined with a reform of the conceptual
approaches to security policies. There has been a growing, if diverse,
body of literature, not entirely from the liberal point of view, arguing
that excessive bureaucracy, emphasis on management and administrative skills over traditional military and combat skills, fascination with
technology over function, and other shortcomings have undermined
the capabilities of the U.S. military establishment in the years since the
Second World War. The Reagan Administration emphasis on more
money without doctrinal change, or even probing exploration, has
fuelled this sort of criticism.

The Reagan–Weinberger approach of more of everything has been
combined with certain emphases, which tend to antagonize different

sorts of reformers. Many professional strategists are concerned about spending which seems to run across the spectrum of possibilities, with no clear sense of priorities. But in the context of overall expansion more money is being spent on some things than on others, even in the specific context of strategic-weapons systems. A lead article in the *Wall Street Journal* toward the end of the fourth year of the Reagan Administration, for example, put the case this way: 'The Reagan buildup hasn't been so much an across the board expansion of U. S. forces as a dramatic investment in strategic nuclear forces and in the Navy, with lesser modernization elsewhere.' Weapons clearly were favoured over wages and salaries, and large, often exotic, systems over others. As time went on, it became clear how long it was taking to produce and deploy these new systems. Ironically, much of the increase in numbers of major weapons was the result of actions in the Carter Administration:

> The Navy has received 93 ships in the last four years, but 86 of these were authorized in the Carter administration. . . . Increasingly, lawmakers worry that there will be a painful spending crunch in the next few years as the Pentagon completes these programs while Congress holds down overall spending to reduce federal deficits.[23]

President Reagan has from time to time called for dramatic arms-reduction efforts, which underscores the inescapability of the nuclear race for Nato as well as for the two superpowers. Because these proposals generally have been delivered in public to the media, they have tended simultaneously to reassure his supporters and irritate his opponents in the United States and overseas. In November 1981, the so-called 'zero–zero' option was introduced, in which the Americans proposed to cancel planned deployments of Pershing II and cruise missiles if the Soviets would withdraw SS-20 and also SS-4 and SS-5 missiles.

In May 1982, with President Reagan's commencement address at Eureka College, the Administration formally proposed the Start (Strategic Arms Reduction Talks) concepts as a successor to the Salt strategy which had guided U.S. arms-control planning and negotiation for approximately a decade. In the words of Richard Burt, a principal spokesman and influential policy-maker in the Reagan Administration,

> The most basic fault of Salt II was the fact that it would permit

substantial growth in both sides' strategic forces, rather than man-
datory reductions. . . . Another major shortcoming was the fact
that Salt II's unit of account was the launcher; no direct limitations
were applied to the number of warheads permitted each side. . . .[24]

In one sense, Start was the latest, and politically most potent, effort
to try to escape the paradox of Mutual Assured Destruction (Mad), the
strategy which had underpinned U.S. nuclear-weapons policy since
the Kennedy Administration. That strategy has rested on the argument that general war could only be deterred if the societies of both
superpowers would be utterly destroyed in a nuclear exchange. Criticism of the Salt I agreements gave considerably greater, and in many
cases quite influential, support to the existing movement, generally
dominated by conservatives, to find some alternative to Mad. Yet
finding an alternative approach with any broad support has been a
most vexing process.

Strategist Jan Lodal, writing in 1980, described the situation thus:

> One might imagine that a strategy that has changed so little after so
> many years would need little revision. Yet the calls for revision are
> in fact growing. . . . Only recently Henry Kissinger wrote: 'Achiev-
> ing a more discriminating nuclear strategy, preserving at least some
> hope for civilized life, remains . . . one of the most difficult tasks
> . . .'. That Kissinger could have made such a statement–given the
> positions he held for eight years, and the influence he exercised
> during that time–suggests how difficult and frustrating a problem it
> is.[25]

The United States proposed a two-stage process of strategic reductions under the Start rubric. During the first phase, it was suggested,
the number of ballistic-missile warheads should be reduced by one
third, to approximately 5000 for each side. Of these, no more than half
would be placed on ICBMs. The United States also proposed cutting
the number of ICBMs to 850. During the second phase, there would
be a substantial cut in the total strategic forces of each side, including a
reduction in missile throw weights and payloads, indices of destructive
capabilities more precise than counting launchers. The proposals represented a dramatic departure from the conventional wisdom, but did
not for that reason produce negative reactions from the U.S. arms-
control establishment. An article in *Arms Control Today* praised the
proposals for their 'straightforward simplicity'.[26]

Meanwhile, the Nato deployments of Pershing II and cruise missiles under the two-track decision proceeded apace, bringing controversy but not major damage to the Alliance. Uncertainty about the deployment reflected insecurity over European commitment to the Alliance. Congressman Lee Hamilton, chairman of the House Foreign Affairs Committee's sub-committee on Europe and the Middle East, stated in the context of releasing a new study on theatre nuclear forces,

> Some steps to implement the 1979 decision to deploy LRTNF [Long Range Tactical Nuclear Forces] are being taken in Europe, but the uncertainty surrounding the prospects for arms control makes final and complete modernization of Nato's theater weapons problematical. Two allies, Belgium and the Netherlands, have agreed in principle with the need for new theater nuclear systems, but are reluctant to approve actual deployment. This situation remains a source of political alliance friction.[27]

The debate over the wisdom of deploying the new missiles continued. Critics, who were not just on the left, charged that in purely military terms the missiles added little or nothing while bringing fresh tensions into the Alliance. For instance, McGeorge Bundy was quoted to this effect in the *New York Times* in late 1981:

> We could hit any targets we would need to hit in the western part of the Soviet Union with the strategic forces already assigned to Nato, in the first instance, the Poseidon submarine. We could hit them with the oncoming force of cruise missiles from bombers, whether the B-52 or a new bomber. We could hit them with the sea-launched cruise missiles projected in the Reagan forces. We can also hit them, although this is a less likely choice, with ICBMs.

In the same piece, Richard Perle, Assistant Secretary of Defense for International Security Policy, defended the Administration's policy, stressing the importance of reliability and continuity:

> The basing of ground-launched missiles in several countries of the alliance is an expression of alliance solidarity. It reflects a willingness to share the risks and burdens of providing for a defense against Soviet nuclear weapons that can't be accomplished with the existing systems. To put it differently, forces seen on the land in Europe

have an inherent credibility that forces more distant and invisible simply can't match.[28]

While Perle stressed the strategic advantages of the new land-based weapons, by the time this interchange appeared in the *New York Times* political considerations had clearly become paramount. Hamilton had identified the nub of the issue – Alliance confidence, related to a test of commitment through willingness to accept the new deployments.

The major exception has been the Strategic Defense Initiative, the so-called 'Star Wars' programme, of the Administration. This has enormously complicated Alliance relations without so far any particular benefit resulting. The S.D.I. has been decidedly controversial even within the United States, so there should be no great surprise that relations with European allies have been complicated as well. The effort flies directly in the face of Mutual Assured Destruction, the doctrine which has guided deterrence policy explicitly since the 1960s. The idea of complex defensive systems to destroy offensive weapons was rejected by earlier U.S. policy-makers, most notably in the Nixon Administration, on the then persuasive grounds that the offence could be enhanced comparatively easily to overwhelm the proposed new defensive capabilities. This time such arguments are still being made but have generally been rejected by those in power.

The Europeans have been concerned that the S.D.I. will greatly stimulate the arms race without providing any positive benefit to the security of the West. The complex arrays of laser and other weapons planned must work with great accuracy and reliability – far more than required of offensive strategic nuclear forces – if they are to succeed in a wartime situation. The implausibility of this happening in turn undermines the credibility of the S.D.I. in the period before war breaks out – in precisely the period when believable deterrence is vital. There are also some basic internal inconsistencies in the initiative, not least the emphasis on space platforms of the sort that will precisely be particularly vulnerable to the new laser weapons being developed.

Also, for Europeans, the S.D.I. effort can be taken to imply a comparative lack of interest in Alliance matters, a return to something resembling a 'fortress America' emphasis. This has been a second major source of concern for them about the new systems. Europeans have argued that the effort will undermine Alliance relations because the Americans will in effect be focusing much more on national security at the price of broader regional concerns.

Europeans have worried that the Star Wars programme will in effect kill whatever chances might exist for genuine arms-control accords between the two superpowers. This is by no means a sentiment limited there to the political left. For instance, Volker Rühe, of Helmut Kohl's Christian Democratic coalition in West Germany, was quoted early in 1985 to the effect that 'The West should make clear that the removal of existing weapons is much more urgent for people than the preoccupation with futuristic visions.' Relatedly, Europeans are concerned that a Soviet effort to counter the new American systems would render their nuclear forces rather inconsequential. Jonathan Alford of the International Institute for Strategic Studies in London has remarked in making this point that 'the consequences for Europe of a Soviet defence initiative would be quite profound' for this reason.[29]

Europeans have also of course complained about the absence of progress in arms-control discussions with the Soviets during the Reagan Administration. As in the United States, there are critics who charge that this reflects a reality in which the Americans really are not that interested in the arms-control process. Despite hostility to President Carter, the Salt II treaty was widely viewed as a base upon which additional accords, addressed specifically to intermediate-range nuclear forces (I.N.F.) based in Europe, could be negotiated. At the end of 1983, however, the Soviets walked out of the Geneva talks with the Americans. Neither the strategic nuclear forces talks – the Start effort – nor the I.N.F. talks made any real progress. While principal blame might rightly be placed on the Soviets, the breakdown was a very negative development for relations. If antagonism to the defence and security policies of the Reagan Administration was not limited to parties of the left in Europe, this sector of the ideological spectrum, in combination with the Protestant and Catholic churches, did provide especially harsh criticism of the American priorities and emphases. In Britain and West Germany especially, the anti-nuclear movements of the left were given new life by the conservative administration in Washington.

In this regard, remarks of Horst Ehmke, a prominent figure in the West German Social Democratic Party, are especially interesting as an example of the efforts of a thoughtful leader on the left to reconcile commitments of the European left and the Atlantic Alliance. He stated in a conference on strategic issues in mid-1983 that,

On account of its geographical location, the Federal Republic bears a particularly high risk in the event of a military conflict. For this reason, but also because of its historical and political situation, it is particularly dependent on understanding . . . and has a special interest in cooperation aimed at easing tensions. . . . In the situation in which we find ourselves, renunciation of force adds directly to our security. The renunciation of the use of force also constitutes the core of the policy of detente. . . .

But he also stated,

As regards this process of change, we are, of course, proceeding on the current Nato strategy of flexible response. It continues to be in force until a new and better strategy has been developed and adopted. . . .

The first use of a nuclear weapon can already lead to an uncontrollable escalation ending in a nuclear holocaust.

It is in the light of this realization that we demand that nuclear battlefield weapons be replaced on a step-by-step basis by modern conventional, defensive weapons. . . .[30]

The conclusion of President Reagan's first term provided a troubled, but not entirely negative, portrait of policy. Arms-limitation talks were stalled, perhaps permanently. At the same time, the Administration had not experienced the intense, almost constant, disruptions and crises which had characterized the Carter years. Reagan was able to establish generally positive relations with his counterparts in West European governments. Moreover, even though tensions with the Soviets continued, and were exacerbated by some of the statements and concrete policy steps of the Reagan Administration, there was not a return to the intense Cold War atmosphere of earlier periods. If *détente* had not continued, the competition with the Soviets also has not led yet to a confrontation comparable to the Cuban Missile Crisis of 1962.

6 Conclusion: Present and Future Nato Relationships

The mixed developments that have occurred in the history of Nato provide a series of important lessons. They bear directly upon the future analysis and definition of policies by Washington and other Alliance capitals. Such a statement is no more than the common observation that shrewd analysis of history brings insights useful in the future. The rub is that there is no certainty or guarantee that the lessons drawn are the right ones. A related observation would be that the Europeans should not necessarily draw for their own policy interests the same lessons as the Americans from experiences since the Second World War. There can be very little disagreement with the fundamental point that Western Europe remains essentially dependent upon the United States for defence. This relates only in part to the argument, increasingly heard in the United States for more than a decade, that the Europeans should do more to defend themselves in conventional terms. The larger reality is that only the nuclear arsenal of the United States can counter in political and symbolic terms the nuclear forces of the Soviet Union. Consequently, at the present time as well as early in the Nato partnership, decisions in Washington have unusually significant bearing on the larger Alliance. For this reason, particular attention here has been paid to the dynamic aspects of change in U.S. administrations, and their foreign policies, in discussing Nato relationships.

A basic theme of this discussion of policies and events over time is that the interests of the partners have sometimes been drastically different, and one strength of Nato has been that limited goals have ensured continuity of Alliance institutions and understandings. A corollary of this position would be that there are lots of other

136

competing or incongruent interests which the allies had best leave alone in their common planning and discussion.

Further, one of the most striking lessons to emerge from an examination of the history of Nato is that the policies of the principal partner, the United States, have oscillated over time. Even American administrations with an intense ambition to make a significant mark in international affairs have had different conceptions of the Atlantic area and European arena. For the Kennedy Administration, Atlantic relations were of paramount importance and, as a result, sweeping goals for a community of the nations involved were pursued. For Nixon and Kissinger, superpower relations were far more important than those with allies, and accordingly Europe was neglected in priority foreign-policy terms. Continued discussion of the approaches of different administrations in the context of Atlantic Alliance relations is one way of underscoring the unpredictability of style and priorities, and specific policies, from one regime to the next.

The purpose of this study is not to provide an exhaustive series of recommendations for policy, or even a complete analysis of events. Rather, the purpose has been to provide sufficient information about the course of events, especially from the viewpoint of Washington, to make some accurate current generalizations about the state of the Alliance and identify sensible policy directions for the future. Some lessons do emerge with some clarity as a result of this approach.

First, in many ways the most striking lesson of the history of the Alliance is that, beyond collegial rhetoric and the good intentions of policy-players, there is no way to escape Nato crises of one sort or another. Equally important, recent problems have not been worse than earlier ones. The Alliance inevitably involves tensions and strains among the partners. Probably the most serious crisis to have afflicted the Alliance was the decisive move of President Eisenhower to deny American assistance to the joint British, French and Israeli strike against Egypt following the takeover of the Suez Canal, and the positive pressure exerted by Washington to bring the adventure to an end. Governments fell, careers were ended and Eisenhower achieved a smashing re-election victory in 1956, a result which might well have been different had he been less decisive in preserving his image at home as the president who had kept the peace.

Domestic political calculations probably were not crucial for Eisenhower – the crucial factor was the undertaking of a secret operation to which the President and Dulles were basically opposed – but they were one part of the calculus in Washington. Since then, the Alliance has faced various challenges, but no worse crisis in terms of basic national differences of view on vital interests or the impact of electoral considerations in one nation on the perceived diplomatic interests of others. Hence, Nato crises are not only nothing new: there is good evidence that they have not grown at all worse over time as the Alliance has aged. The fact that one constant in US foreign policy has been competition among players in any particular administration, and disagreement concerning even basic mechanisms for co-ordination, argues that uncertainty in relations with European allies cannot be avoided.

Second, Nato has faced a series of national disruptions of the transnational plan. Rather than seeing these as automatically unwelcome, they should again be recognized as virtually inevitable, and American foreign-policy planning in particular should try as much as possible to anticipate them. There is much to be said for national independence within the context of the Alliance. The Franco-German treaty of 1963, as Kennedy had the insight to appreciate, frustrated American policy in the short term, especially in view of the intense and rather theatrical competition with de Gaulle, but was congruent with longer-term mutual interests in binding the West Germans more intricately to the wider Western community. De Gaulle's own independent foreign policy, succeeded by the paler, less imaginative imitation provided by Giscard d'Estaing, irritated Washington and lent a decidedly dramatic tone to Atlantic relations during the Kennedy Administration, but also served to create and preserve French national identity and domestic stability following years in which the political culture of that country had enjoyed neither quality.

Again, there is nothing new about this but the point has not always been appreciated in U.S. foreign policy. De Gaulle as President of France in the fifth Republic, while clearly a distinctive and perhaps unique leader, was eccentric to be sure. But he also personified an urge for national definition which was extremely important for his nation in the face of the military humiliation and political instability of the 1940s and 1950s. Arguably France is a special case, given the trauma of Vichy combined with the promise of national renewal represented by President de Gaulle. Yet national commitment remains a vital ingredient of political life in Europe. It is without doubt characteristic of all the nations in Nato, especially the major players, and perhaps the West Germans most of all. The fact that the European Community has in fact failed to undercut fundamental national sovereignty, that economic integration and co-ordination of certain technical functions has not interfered with basic political sovereignty, underscores the strength of the national kernels. The sentiments so popular among many informed people in the early 1960s, to the effect that a kind of European superstate was emerging, to be combined with North America in a grand Atlantic community, seem visionary indeed from the view point of the 1980s.

In this context, as in others, Nato policy has a particular requirement to understand the dictates of realism. This is especially important for an alliance so inclusive and so old. For both reasons, there is fragility to the structure. Complacency may mean that even minor crises and misunderstandings shake the foundations of the Alliance. The passage of time and movement of events presumably will put new pressures on the structure; to some extent they already have done so. The involvement of so many nations in the Alliance, a fundamental reality now as at the founding of Nato, means that consensus, and the inevitable handmaiden caution, are unavoidable if policy is to be both clearly defined and expected to work.

Third, the Alliance has been successful primarily because conflicts in third areas of the world, outside the primary parameters of the Alliance, have been ruled out. Informal consultation has on occasion been helpful. Certainly Eisenhower's refusal in 1954 to do more to assist the French in Indochina without more general concurrence from the allies was crucial in keeping the United States out of the morass at that time. The United States might have benefitted from more open consultation with European allies before the major escalation in Vietnam in 1965. There was good, but explicitly limited, co-operation between the United States and Nato allies when American transport aircraft were used to carry French and Belgian paratroopers to the rescue of European civilians in Zaire in the late 1970s. Likewise, American logistical support, we now know, was vital to British success in the Falklands War with Argentina in the early 1980s. Yet these and other examples of good co-operation in third areas were decidedly specific, *ad hoc* and not part of a more general, regular Alliance policy or design.

This argues, among other things, for keeping the Japanese from having a more substantial direct role in Nato. The notion of greater Nato involvement in third areas of conflict was encouraged primarily by developments in the Middle East, and in particular by the sense of shared dependency on oil resources there on the part of the industrialized nations. However, the point bears in the most telling manner on relations with Japan, especially those of Washington but also those of the European allies. The waning of the oil–energy crises of the 1970s, with plentiful supplies and a resulting downward trend in price, has perhaps led to complacency which will be dangerous over the longer term. However, the basic point remains that, whether there is oil shortage or oil surplus in terms of the needs of the industrial states, whatever oil security policies – if any – are decided upon collectively by Western nations should be handled outside the context of Nato. Security conflicts and related developments outside the Atlantic area, political and economic as well as military, have a bearing upon the Alliance, sometimes with very important consequences. Nevertheless, pressing to use the Nato structure to address third-area military or economic challenges can only have a negative effect on the cohesion of this old, but still fragile, security understanding.

Fourth, there is much which can be done in the area of technical, tactical, organizational and administrative improvements to help to bind the Alliance more closely together. Alexander Haig's record here as Nato commander during the Carter Administration provides a good record which can be emulated and upon which to build. This is a promising area in part because the issues are basically technical and apolitical in nature. The S.D.I., which has fostered so much fresh tension within Nato, ironically provides an opportunity to use technical co-operation as a device for Alliance solidarity. This exceptionally expensive programme should, for that very reason, provide a range of opportunities for co-operation at least in terms of American procurement contracts let to European companies.

More directly, in terms of military units in the field, Nato not only provides opportunity in principle but demonstration in fact that military necessity provides levers for enhanced Alliance co-operation. While the Reagan Administration has been criticized for defence programming which involves considerably more spending without much conceptual guidance, Nato practical military co-operation has moved in progressive areas of change. While Defense Secretary Weinberger defends his flanks, and front, from increasingly serious political attacks from Congress and elsewhere, General Bernard Rogers, Haig's successor in Europe, has moved rather quietly significantly to reform and reinforce Nato's capabilities.

This effort builds upon but goes beyond earlier initiatives. Haig emphasized organizational mechanisms and such factors as inter-operability and standardization of weapons and equipment. Essentially, Rogers and his staff have engaged in much more comprehensive planning, which has updated the tenet that effective defence includes attention to the offence. 'Deep strike' is one of several terms applied to a new emphasis on the use of precision-guided, advanced-technology weapons to break up Warsaw Pact attacks in the event of war in Europe, to include penetration into Eastern Europe to destroy crucial bridges, roads, airfields, supply depots and troop concentrations. The approach includes a focus on brigade-level and smaller units, downplaying earlier stress on division-level control and use of firepower to hammer an enemy. The new doctrinal activity, closely linked to actual plans, has revitalized Nato in the field at a time when Washington's defence-policy efforts have been moving in different, less imaginative directions.[1]

One very important consideration, especially at a time when the U.S. Congress apparently has reached the limit of its support for expanded defence spending, is that the Rogers plan does not involve substantial fresh expenditures. As with Haig's earlier effort to counter Soviet tanks with U.S. anti-tank weapons, notably the T.O.W. (Tube-launched, Optically-tracked, Wire-guided) missile, which are substantially less expensive, the current Nato commander is stressing doctrinal shifts which do not require enormous new spending on weapons or equipment. Precision-guided munitions, a basic technical advance of the 1970s which greatly enhances the accuracy of projectiles in reaching the target, open the door to design and development of a range of new weapons which will be much less expensive than the tanks, aircraft, ships and other targets they can destroy with great reliability.

This state of affairs has implications beyond the need to respect national sentiments and independence within the security umbrella. Among other things, it means that the American commitment has to be constantly reaffirmed. A basic initial purpose of Nato was to represent without confusion or ambiguity the fundamental American security stake in Western Europe. Historically, the natural inclinations of the United States have been to move in the reverse direction where European (though not Latin American or even Asian) commitments are concerned.

In turn, reasoning on this basis argues for keeping the *status quo* in broad policy rather than pursuing fundamental shifts in the purposes or structure of the Alliance. Europeans can be pressed to 'do more' for collective defence, but one lesson of reviewing Alliance history is that they already do a lot. And any basic shift in the *status quo* could have various unintended consequences.

American troop reductions in Europe are a perennial subject for

discussion. Hence, the recent proposal in *Foreign Affairs* by Earl
Ravenal, reflecting a wider debate, for a drastic reduction of the
American troop levels in Western Europe, as a way of forcing the allies
to accept responsibility for their own defence, is in line with a series of
proposals in this vein reaching back to the Eisenhower years.[2] While
the economic balance between Europe and the United States has
shifted drastically over the past four decades, the reality of heavy
Soviet power virtually on the border of Western Europe has not.
Moving large numbers of US forces back across the Atlantic, whether
proposed now as part of the effort to foster European responsibility, or
in earlier years as part of such proposals as the nuclear-free zone in
central Europe, would inevitably dilute the Alliance, encourage pressure from the still proximate Soviets, and contain no guarantee that the
West Europeans would necessarily do more for their own national or
regional defence. The troops were sent there initially not primarily in
response to the inherent economic weakness of Europe, but as testimony to changed American security sentiments in the face of Soviet
control of Eastern Europe.

Reasoning in these terms leads to the conclusion that the policy
openings in the context of Europe most likely to bring useful results
will be tactical rather than strategic in nature, and technical rather than
political. This is why Generals Haig and Rogers have been able, with
administrative drive and diplomatic skill, to make significant positive
reforms in such important (if undramatic) areas as weapons and equipment modernization, and the doctrines by which Nato would be guided
if war actually breaks out in Europe. This is also why U.S. government
leaders, and those of other European countries as well as the Soviet
Union, have been so singularly unsuccessful in bringing about breakthroughs of a more profoundly political kind.

Nato is such an old alliance, and the situation in Europe so frozen,
not because of a lack of diplomatic effort but as a reflection of structural requirements which have remained virtually unchanged for
nearly four decades. Given Soviet postures, and the frigid relations
between the two camps during the Reagan Administration, this basic
state of affairs is unlikely to change – at least, not in a direction positive
for American and West European interests – over the next few years.
Yet this is not necessarily a depressing situation. Nato has survived so
extraordinarily long precisely because it has served effectively the
combined interest of the nations involved. By surviving as a function-
ing organization, representing therefore a viable source of military

response in the event of attack, the Alliance has helped to avoid a general war in Europe. Europe at peace for forty years is an exceptional state of affairs, not just in the context of the twentieth century, and should be recognized as such.

Notes

CHAPTER 1. INTRODUCTION

1. *Newsweek,* 2 June 1980, p. 49.
2. *Newsweek,* 19 May 1980, p. 108.

CHAPTER 2. THE ANCIENT ALLIANCE

1. Hans J. Morgenthau, *Politics in the Twentieth Century: The Restoration of American Politics* (Chicago: University of Chicago Press, 1962) p. 329, quoted in Kenneth W. Thompson, *Cold War Theories,* I: *World Polarization, 1943–1953* (Baton Rouge and London: Louisiana State University Press, 1981) p. 114.
2. See the interesting, well-written discussion in Thompson (ibid., pp.123–6).
3. A. W. DePorte, *Europe between the Superpowers – the Enduring Balance* (New Haven, Conn. and London: Yale University Press, 1979) p. 12.
4. See, for example, Max Beloff, *The United States and the Unity of Europe* (New York: Vintage Books, 1963) pp. 9–11.
5. Escott Reid, 'The Miraculous Birth of the North Atlantic Alliance', *Nato Review,* no. 6 (Dec 1980) pp. 14, 17.
6. Walter Lippmann, 'Britain and America: The Prospects of Political Cooperation in Light of their Paramount Interests', *Foreign Affairs,* 13, no. 3 (Apr 1935) p. 371.
7. Paul Seabury, *The Rise and Decline of the Cold War* (New York and London: Basic Books, 1967) pp. 28–9
8. Ibid., p. 17.
9. David N. Schwartz, *Nato's Nuclear Dilemmas* (Washington, DC: Brookings Institution, 1983) p. 8.
10. Samuel Flagg Bemis, *A Diplomatic History of the United States* (New York: Holt, Rinehart and Winston, 1947) pp. 927, 929.
11. On Kennan's attitudes and alternative approaches toward Europe, with sensitivity to Eastern Europe, see Beloff, *The United States and the Unity of Europe,* pp. 73–4.
12. See, for example, Dean Acheson, *Present at the Creation – My Years in the State Department* (New York: W. W. Norton, 1969) pp. 354–61, 414–25.
13. Ibid., p. 358.
14. Bemis, *A Diplomatic History of the United States,* pp. 946–7.

15. Townsend Hoopes, *The Devil and John Foster Dulles* (Boston, Mass.: Little, Brown, 1973) chs 21–3.
16. Ibid., p. 374.
17. Ibid., p. 375.
18. Ibid., p. 385.
19. Catherine McArdle Kelleher, *Germany and the Politics of Nuclear Weapons* (New York and London: Columbia University Press, 1975) p. 31.
20. Ibid., p. 43.
21. Hoopes, *The Devil and Dulles*, p. 313.
22. Ibid., p. 460.
23. Theodore H. White, *The Making of the President 1960* (New York: Atheneum, 1961) p. 117.

CHAPTER 3.   NEW STRATEGIES, NEW STRATEGISTS

1. White, in *The Making of the President*, is clearly partisan regarding Kennedy and presents a most positive view of his presidential campaign. Concerning the Kennedy Administration, the most interesting and informative of the partisan biographies is probably Arthur Schlesinger, Jr, *A Thousand Days – John F. Kennedy in the White House* (Boston, Mass.: Houghton Mifflin, 1965).
2. 'As one aide later put it, "For Mac Bundy, the world was Europe, and Europe was the United Kingdom, Germany, France and Russia." So it was in his interest to have congenial associates brief Kennedy on other areas. . . . When Kennedy kept asking Bundy for briefings about the war in Yemen, the Special Assistant would respond, "Don't ask me, ask Komer"' – I. M. Destler, Leslie H. Gelb and Anthony Lake, *Our Own Worst Enemy – The Unmaking of American Foreign Policy* (New York: Simon and Schuster, 1984) p. 190.
3. David Halberstam's principal book about the Vietnam War is perhaps best and most accurate concerning the tone and atmosphere of those times: 'Yet if there was a problem with the pragmatism of the period, it was that there were simply too many foreign policy problems, too many crises, each crowding the others, demanding to be taken care of in that instant. There was too little time to plan, to think . . .' – *The Best and the Brightest* (New York: Random House, 1969) p. 102.
4. One of the most imaginative treatments, thorough yet comparatively brief, in part because of use of quantitative analysis, is Arnold Kanter, *Defense Politics – A Budgetary Perspective* (Chicago and London: University of Chicago Press, 1975). See also James Fallows, *National Defense* (New York: Vintage Books, 1981). His book is a harsh critique of US weapons and the system that produces them, but he also states, 'There is much to admire in Robert McNamara's record. For instance, he ran the Pentagon, instead of being run by it. If there is a surprising degree of residual bitterness toward him among professional military men, much of it comes from their frustration that McNamara was so effective in making civilian control work' (p. 20).

5. ' "If we are to assure that the disastrous big war never occurs," as Taylor put it, "we must have the means to deter or to win the small wars" ' – Schlesinger, *A Thousand Days*, p. 310. The emphasis on conventional – and unconventional – warfare preparation dovetailed with influential approaches in the academic world: 'Nor was the Army the only advocate of conventional defense. As early as 1950, a group of eleven Harvard and M.I.T. faculty members – including McGeorge Bundy, John Kenneth Galbraith, Arthur Schlesinger, Jerome Weisner and Herrold Zacharias – had written a long letter to *The New York Times* criticizing on moral and strategic grounds the military establishment's predominant reliance on atomic warfare' – Fred Kaplan, *The Wizards of Armageddon* (New York: Simon and Schuster, 1983) p. 195.
6. Schlesinger, *A Thousand Days*, pp. 500–1.
7. Richard E. Neustadt, *Alliance Politics* (New York and London: Columbia University Press, 1970) esp. pp. 47ff.
8. Beloff, *The United States and the Unity of Europe*, p. 161.
9. Henry A. Kissinger, *The Troubled Partnership: A Re-appraisal of the Atlantic Alliance* (Garden City, NY: Anchor Books, Doubleday, 1965) p. 160.
10. Ibid., p. 141.
11. See ibid., esp. chs 5 and 6, for one of the earliest and most telling critiques of American efforts at dominance in Alliance nuclear-weapons policies.
12. Richard E. Neustadt, *Presidential Power* (New York: John Wiley, 1964) pp. 186–7.
13. John Baylis, *Anglo-American Defence Relations 1939–1980: The Special Relationship* (New York: St Martin's Press, 1981) pp. 68–9.
14. Ibid., p. 71; quote from Kissinger, *The Troubled Partnership*, p. 80.
15. Baylis, *Anglo–American Defence Relations*, p. 45.
16. Ibid., pp. 44–5.
17. Desmond Ball, *Politics and Force Levels – The Strategic Missile Program of the Kennedy Administration* (Berkeley, Los Angeles and London: University of California Press, 1980) pp. 4–5.
18. Ibid., p. xxi
19. Ball (ibid., pp. 18, 21 and *passim*) develops this theme, including the ambiguity concerning Kennedy's own belief in his missile gap claims.
20. Schlesinger, *A Thousand Days*, pp. 375–8, 816.
21. Neustadt, *Alliance Politics*, pp. 54–5.
22. See, for example, Hans Morgenthau, *Politics among Nations* (New York: Alfred Knopf, 1948) pp. 187ff.
23. 'There is reason to believe that Khrushchev took Kennedy's measure at their Vienna meeting in June 1961, and decided this was a young man who would shrink from hard decisions'; 'Kennedy said just enough in that room in the embassy to convince me of the following: Khrushchev had studied the events of the Bay of Pigs . . . decided he was dealing with an inexperienced young leader who could be intimidated and black-mailed. The Communist decision to put offensive missiles into Cuba was the final gamble of this assumption' – statements respectively by Elie Abel and James Reston, from Abel, *The Cuban Missile Crisis*

(Philadelphia: Walter Lippincott, 1966) pp. 35ff.
24. Schlesinger, *A Thousand Days*, p. 871.

CHAPTER 4.   THE GLOBAL REACH OF GREAT POWER

1. Kelleher, *Germany and the Politics of Nuclear Weapons*, p. 357. This book provides an unusually clear and thorough analysis of the M.L.F. events.
2. Ibid., pp. 240, 245.
3. Ibid., p. 254.
4. Ibid., p. 260.
5. Ibid., p. 263.
6. Alfred Grosser, *The Western Alliance – European–American Relations since 1945* (New York: Continuum, 1980) p. 213.
7. Schlesinger, in *A Thousand Days*, esp. chs 34 and 37, provides an informative discussion of the evolution of US–Soviet security relations in the early 1960s.
8. Seabury, *The Rise and Decline of the Cold War*, p. 109.
9. Grosser, *The Western Alliance*, pp. 213–14.
10. Ibid., p. 214.
11. Ibid., p. 217.
12. Ibid., p. 221.
13. One stimulating discussion of the decline of the post-war system of economic relations with special reference to Atlantic-area relations is provided by Benjamin J. Cohen: 'The Revolution in Atlantic Economic Relations: A Bargain Comes Unstuck', in Wolfram F. Hanreider (ed.), *The United States and Western Europe* (Cambridge, Mass.: Winthrop, 1974) pp. 106–33.
14. Grosser, *The Western Alliance*, p. 236.
15. One detailed, perceptive discussion of the elements of the crisis is provided by John Newhouse's *Collision in Brussels* (New York: W. W. Norton, 1967).
16. See, for example, Stanley Hoffmann, *Gulliver's Troubles – Or the Setting of American Foreign Policy* (New York: McGraw-Hill, 1968) *passim*, ch. 12.
17. Peter Merkl, *German Foreign Policies, West and East* (Santa Barbara, Calif., and Oxford: ABC Clio Press, 1974) p. 118.
18. See Grosser, *The Western Alliance*, p. 232, on the factors in Erhard's fall.
19. Merkl, *German Foreign Policies*, p. 121.
20. Ibid.
21. Ibid., p. 123.
22. Ibid., p. 124.
23. Ibid., pp. 126–7.
24. Ibid., pp. 134, 150.
25. Baylis, *Anglo-American Defence Relations*, pp. 79–80.
26. Ibid., pp. 85–91.
27. Ibid., pp. 118ff.

28. Ibid., pp. 91–2.
29. Ibid., p. 95.
30. Grosser, *The Western Alliance*, p. 239.
31. Perhaps the most perceptive study of efforts to achieve peace, or at least de-escalation, in Vietnam during the Johnson Administration is David Kraslow and Stuart H. Loory, *The Secret Search for Peace in Vietnam* (New York: Vintage Books, 1968) *passim*.
32. Arthur Cyr, *British Foreign Policy and the Atlantic Area – The Techniques of Accommodation* (London: Macmillan, 1979) pp. 73–4.
33. Henry A. Kissinger, *White House Years* (Boston, Mass., and Toronto: Little, Brown, 1979) pp. 412ff. From p. 413: 'In the Harmel Report to Nato of December 1967, named after the Belgian Foreign Minister, therefore, the Alliance put the collective search for "progress towards a more stable relationship" with Eastern Europe high on its list of priorities, second only to deterrence of aggression. In June 1968 at the meeting of its Foreign Ministers in Reykjavik, Nato signalled its readiness to discuss mutual and balanced force reductions (M.B.F.R.) – the new technical term for disengagement – with the Warsaw Pact.'
34. See ibid., pp. 126, 552, on Nixon's intense worry about Glassboro.
35. One of the most interesting and thorough treatments of the problems of U.S. government organization for foreign policy is I. M. Destler, *Presidents, Bureaucrats and Foreign Policy* (Princeton, NJ: Princeton University Press, 1974), esp the Epilogue on the Nixon system.
36. Eric F. Goldman, *The Tragedy of Lyndon Johnson* (New York: Alfred A. Knopf, 1969) p. 275.
37. Some have also emphasized that the British were actually rather similar to the French in their overt suspicion of independent European supranational political authority. See, for example, F. Roy Willis, 'Germany, France and Europe', in Wolfram F. Hanrieder (ed.), *West German Foreign Policy: 1949–1979* (Boulder, Col.: Westview Press, 1980) pp. 103–4.
38. Cyr, *British Foreign Policy*, pp. 74–5.
39. Kissinger, *White House Years*, p. 410.
40. See, for example, Grosser, *The Western Alliance*, p. 288: 'during the final phase of the conference, the Europeans repeatedly managed to reach genuine unity and to speak with a single voice. Perhaps this was possible because the issue at stake was not very important. . . . '
41. See, for example, David A. Walker, 'Some Underlying Problems for International Monetary Reform', and Edward L. Morse, 'European Monetary Union and American Foreign Economic Policy', in Hanrieder, *The United States and Western Europe*, pp. 164–210.

CHAPTER 5.   DISCONTINUITY, UNCERTAINTY AND CHANGE: ATLANTICISM IN RETREAT

1. Jimmy Carter, *Keeping Faith – Memoirs of a President* (New York: Bantam Books, 1982) p. 150.
2. Jimmy Carter, *The Blood of Abraham – Insights into the Middle East*

(Boston, Mass.: Houghton Mifflin, 1985) *passim*, and esp. pp. 50–1, 169; see also *Keeping Faith*, pp. 405–6.

3. Carter, *Keeping Faith*, p. 54.
4. Ibid., p. 52.
5. Ibid., pp. 536–7.
6. John Vinocur, 'The Schmidt Factor', *New York Times Magazine*, 21 Sept 1980, p. 112.
7. James O. Goldsborough, 'Europe Cashes in on Carter's Cold War', *New York Times Magazine*, 27 Apr 1980, p. 42.
8. *Wall Street Journal*, 2 Jan 1979, p. 6.
9. *Atlantic Community News*, May 1979, p. 3. Success with Nato on the two-track decision should not overshadow the considerable frustration Washington experienced in trying to persuade European allies to co-operate in the trade boycott of the Soviet Union. Despite Carter's call for a grain and high-technology boycott of the Soviets, West German companies went ahead and tripled their grain sales to them. Major new trading-contracts were signed with the Soviet Union during the period that the Americans were urging boycott. See, for example, *Wall Street Journal*, 20 May 1981, p. 16. While West Europeans condemned the Soviet invasion of Afghanistan, they agreed in specific terms only to refrain from taking advantage of the U.S. boycott by increasing their own exports. They refused to cut back their own trade with that country. *New York Times*, 4 Feb 1980, p. 19.
10. *New York Times*, 7 Oct 1979, p. 13.
11. *New York Times*, 2 Mar 1980, p.36.
12. *New York Times*, 7 Oct 1979, p. 1; *Time*, 24 Dec 1979, p. 30.
13. *Washington Star*, 13 Mar 1979.
14. Quoted in, 'French Embassy, Press and Information Division', PP/79/9.
15. Carter, *Keeping Faith*, pp. 444, 449.
16. Ibid., p. 450.
17. *New York Times*, 25 May 1980, p. 3.
18. *New York Times*, 4 Mar 1981, p. 4.
19. *Time*, 16 Mar 1981, p. 12.
20. Nil Ozergene, *Lessons of the Pipeline Negotiations*, A.C.I.S. (University of California at Los Angeles, Center for Arms Control and International Security) Working Paper no. 40, p. 28 and *passim*.
21. *Wall Street Journal*, 1 Apr 1981, p. 1.
22. *Atlantic Community News*, Feb 1981, p. 1.
23. *Wall Street Journal*, 19 Oct 1984, p. 1.
24. Richard Burt, 'The Evolution of the U. S. START Approach', *Nato Review*, 30, no. 4 (Sep 1982) p. 4.
25. Jan Lodal, 'Deterrence and Nuclear Strategy', *Daedalus*, 109, no. 4 (Fall 1980) p. 157.
26. Gil Klinger and Herbert Scoville, Jr, 'The Politics and Strategy of Start', *Arms Control Today*, 12, no. 7 (July–Aug 1982) p. 4.
27. *Atlantic Community News*, Feb 1981, p. 4.
28. *New York Times*, 22 Nov 1981, p. 2E.
29. Quoted in the *Wall Street Journal*, 8 Jan 1985, p. 39.
30. 'Remarks by Horst Ehmke at the European–American Conference of

the Friedrich Ebert Foundation ', Bonn, 23–4 June 1983, pp. 6, 8, 10.

CHAPTER 6.   CONCLUSION; PRESENT AND FUTURE NATO
RELATIONSHIPS

1. *Strategic Survey*, published by the International Institute of Strategic Studies, regularly provides the most thorough review of political as well as military developments bearing on the Alliance and regional relations more generally. See, for example, the 1984–5 volume (London: International Institute for Strategic Studies, 1985) pp. 45–55.
2. Earl C. Ravenal, 'Europe Without America', *Foreign Affairs*, 63, no. 5 (Summer 1985) pp. 1020–35. The issue has been further complicated by the debate over no first use of nuclear weapons in Europe. See especially McGeorge Bundy, George Kennan, Robert McNamara and Gerard Smith, 'Nuclear Weapons and the Alliance', *Foreign Affairs*, 60, no. 4 (Spring 1982) pp. 753–68; and Karl Kaiser, Georg Leber, Alois Mertes and Franz-Josef Schulze, 'Nuclear Weapons and the Preservation of Peace', *Foreign Affairs*, 60, no. 5 (Summer 1982) pp. 1157–70.

On the implications of new technologies and related strategies, one good analysis is provided by Andrew J. Pierre, Richard D. DeLaver, François L. Heisbourg, Andreas von Bülow and General Sir Hugh Beach, *The Conventional Defense of Europe: New Technologies and New Strategies* (New York: Council on Foreign Relations, 1986).

Index